J. R. R. TOLKIEN
Myth, Morality, and Religion

J. R. R. TOLKIEN

Myth, Morality, and Religion

Richard L. Purtill

Harper & Row, Publishers, San Francisco

Cambridge, Hagerstown, New York, Philadelphia

1817   London, Mexico City, São Paulo, Singapore, Sydney

Acknowledgment is made to Houghton Mifflin Company and George Allen & Unwin Publishers Ltd., for permission to quote from *The Letters of J. R. R. Tolkien* edited by Humphrey Carpenter, copyright © 1981 by George Allen & Unwin Publishers Ltd.; *Tolkien: A Biography* by Humphrey Carpenter, copyright © 1977 by George Allen & Unwin Publishers Ltd.; and the following books by J. R. R. Tolkien: *The Tolkien Reader,* copyright © 1966 by J. R. R. Tolkien; *The Hobbit,* copyright © 1966 by J. R. R. Tolkien; *The Fellowship of the Ring,* copyright © 1965 by J. R. R. Tolkien; *The Return of the King,* copyright © 1965 by J. R. R. Tolkien; *The Silmarillion,* copyright © 1977 by George Allen & Unwin Publishers Ltd.; to Dodd, Mead & Company, Inc., A. P. Watt Ltd., and Miss D. E. Collins for permission to quote from "The Ballad of the White Horse" by G. K. Chesterton, from *The Collected Poems of G. K. Chesterton;* to Harcourt Brace Jovanovich, Inc., for permission to quote from *Of Other Worlds* by C. S. Lewis, copyright © 1966 by The Executors of the Estate of C. S. Lewis; to Running Press, 125 S. 22nd Street, Philadelphia, PA 19103, for permission to quote from *The Biography of J. R. R. Tolkien, Architect of Middle Earth* by Daniel Grotta, copyright © 1978 by Running Press.

FIRST EDITION

Library of Congress Cataloging in Publication Data

Purtill, Richard L.

J.R.R. TOLKIEN : MYTH; MORALITY, AND RELIGION.

1. Tolkien, J. R. R. (John Ronald Reuel), 1892–1973—
Criticism and interpretation. 2. Fantastic fiction,
English—History and criticism. 3. Myth in literature.
4. Ethics in literature. 5. Religion in literature.
I. Title. II. Title: JRR Tolkien.
PR6039.032Z795 1984   828'.91209   84-47733
ISBN 0-06-066712-5

84 85 86 87 88 10 9 8 7 6 5 4 3 2 1

This book is dedicated
to all those who love the work of
J. R. R. Tolkien
but especially to the members of
The Mythopoeic Society

Contents

Preface

One of my qualifications for writing this book is a love of my subject. I first encountered J. R. R. Tolkien's *The Hobbit* on a library shelf when I was a child; I can still remember the look and feel of the book. I dipped into it and was immediately enchanted. It became one of my favorite books, and I returned to it periodically for re-reading. I remember the thrill I felt years later when I read in the preface to C. S. Lewis's book *That Hideous Strength,* "Those who would like to learn further about Númenor and the True West must (alas!) await the publication of much that still exists only in the mss. of my friend Professor J. R. R. Tolkien."[1]* There was more, then, of Tolkien's marvelous mythology, and someday it might be published.

It was a long wait—from the forties to the sixties—but eventually I had another encounter on a library shelf: the three hardcover volumes of *The Lord of the Rings.* I remember that I took only the first volume, wondering if the fairy-tale atmosphere that so delighted me in *The Hobbit* could be sustained in so long a work. There was a hurried trip back to the library when I realized how much I was going to enjoy this story, but volumes two and three of the book were still on the shelves: this was before the "Tolkien craze" of the later sixties; indeed, it may have been before the publication of the first paperback editions.

I became a writer about Tolkien when in 1972 I received a summer grant from the National Endowment for the Humanities to do some research and writing. I had asked myself what I would really enjoy spending a summer thinking and writing about, and in my proposal I had outlined a book on Tolkien, C. S. Lewis, and Charles Williams. Williams proved too hard to write about together with the others, but I eventually did write the book: *Lord of the Elves and Eldils: Fantasy and Philosophy in C. S. Lewis and J. R. R. Tolkien.*[2]

When the book was published I found that I had become a "Tolkien

---

*Notes can be found at the end of the book.

scholar," and I was occasionally asked for lectures or papers on Tolkien. In 1979 the Mythopoeic Society, which is dedicated to the study and appreciation of Tolkien, Lewis, and Williams, was kind enough to ask me to be guest of honor at the eighth annual Mythcon, in San Diego. The paper I read to them was the ancestor of Chapter 2 of this book.

I found that I had more to say about both Lewis and Tolkien; I eventually wrote a book on Lewis's apologetics[3] and began thinking about this book. During the period since my work on *Lord of the Elves and Eldils* I have taught, almost every year, a course on Philosophy and Fantasy that examines philosophical ideas in fantasy fiction. Tolkien and Lewis have always been among the authors read and discussed, and I have learned a great deal from discussing them with students.

The publication, within a few years, of *The Silmarillion,* Humphrey Carpenter's biography of Tolkien, and a volume of Tolkien's letters[4] stimulated my own thinking about Tolkien, and this book was the eventual result. The *Letters* especially are filled with fascinating insights into Tolkien's own view of his work, confirming some guesses that could be made from reading his work and refuting other ideas about what he was doing. *The Silmarillion* filled in a good deal of the mythological background that gives such depth and richness to *The Lord of the Rings.*

I have written the present book mainly for other lovers of Tolkien, using what skills I have as a teacher and writer to help them understand better what we both have enjoyed. I have tried to point out some things that the reader may have missed, put other things into perspective, and show interconnections between various parts of Tolkien's work. My hope is that my readers will return to Tolkien with increased understanding and enjoyment; I hope I have not deserved Gandalf's condemnation (which Tolkien applied to some analysts of his work): "He that breaks a thing in order to find out what it is has left the path of wisdom."[5]

Like Tolkien, I am a university professor, mostly teaching subjects not directly related to literature (he was a philologist, I am a logician and metaphysician), and like Tolkien, I have tried my hand at writing fantasy. I once lived in England for several years. I am a Catholic, as Tolkien was, and share some of his experience of the pre-Vatican II church, in England and elsewhere. Of course, in many ways my experiences have been very unlike Tolkien's, but I hope that those experiences we have shared give me insight into, and sympathy with, my subject.

But to return to my main qualification: I am a lover of Tolkien's work. Those who love a person, place, or thing like to share their appreciation with others and help them to greater appreciation. That is what I have tried to do here.

1. The Dimensions of Myth

Myths are stories, but they are more than stories. The stories of Tolkien do not quite attain to the dignity of real myths; but they are something more than stories, and the "something more" is usually, though not always, in the direction of myth. So much has been written about myth, from all kinds of standpoints, with all kinds of purposes, that the boundaries of the concept of myth have been considerably stretched. In one sense of myth, a myth need not even be a story; in another broad sense of myth, the stories of Tolkien easily qualify as myths. So my first job will be to say what I mean by myth and why I say that Tolkien's stories approach but do not attain that status.

Myths in the original, unstretched sense were stories of gods or heroes that usually had a religious or moral purpose. As with any kind of communication, it is useful to look at the intention of the communicator, the context of understanding of the audience, and the form of the communication. When human beings begin to tell myths, they sometimes do so simply because they think, for whatever reason, that the stories are true. But the mythmaker need not think that every detail, or even every important element, of the story is true. Whoever Homer was, he almost certainly believed in the Olympian gods and even in the historical existence of people named Odysseus and Achilles and Penelope and Helen. He presented what *might* have happened to those people, selecting from legends and traditions but also using his own imagination. In some ways his intention was not unlike that of a modern historical novelist, who reconstructs historical events and personages aided by imagination but directed by fact.

However, the original mythmakers did not aim only to tell an interesting story (though it is important to remember that they did intend at least that). They aimed to do something that they would probably have expressed as a desire to *honor* the gods and heroes and to *inspire* their listeners. Their audiences, in turn, looked on the myths as conveying moral and religious lessons; in fact, the telling of and listening to myths could have moral and religious significance. Myths also had a close connection with ritual; they were acted out in ceremonies of various kinds.

The literary form in which myth can be expressed is quite open: simple prose narrative, lyric or epic poetry, and drama are among the forms that have been used. Myth does not exclude humor, but it must be humor of a special kind, as we shall see. Again, to take Homer as a paradigm case of original myth, we find that his literary form is epic poetry. Prose "epitomes" or summaries of Homer were made in later ages by people with an antiquarian interest in myths no longer believed. There is humor, human interest, and excitement in Homer, all of them things that even some very perceptive students of myth have thought incompatible with the mythical dimension. But in classical Greece, where theater was an important way of presenting myth, the short humorous plays that were called satyr plays were regarded as just as appropriate and proper as the tragedies for the presentation of myth.

Original myth, as I will call it, is related to myth in a number of wider senses. On the one side, myth is related to what I will call gospel, which includes but is not confined to the four New Testament accounts. In gospel we have stories of the acts of God and of those close to God —saints rather than heroes. By the traditional believer (Tolkien himself, for instance), gospel is regarded as literally and historically true in all its important elements (and even perhaps in its details). It is specifically denied that human imagination or invention plays any part in gospel as I am using the term. But otherwise gospel resembles original myth in a number of ways. It has religious and moral significance for teller and audience; it can take a wide variety of literary forms; and it has a close connection with ritual. The procession from Athens to Eleusis was explained and justified by the myth of Demeter and Persephone. The celebration of Mass or Holy Communion in Christian churches is explained and justified by the Christian Gospels.

On another side, original myth is related to literary myth, which is the use of mythical characters and heroes for purely literary purposes. Neither the author nor the audience of literary myth regards the story as true, and though religious or moral lessons may be conveyed, they are not conveyed in the way that is characteristic of original myth.

A third relative of original myth that should be briefly noted is philosophical myth, the conveying of philosophical ideas by allegories or metaphors that have a greater or lesser resemblance to original myth. The philosophical ideas are regarded as true, but not the story in which they are embodied. There is no connection to ritual, and even the element of *story* may become very attenuated. Plato's use of philosophical myth in his dialogues is a good paradigm for this kind of myth. For example, in the myth or allegory of the Cave, Plato expresses a philosophical idea about appearance and reality in the form of an image of prisoners chained in a cave and observing real objects only by the shadows they cast on the wall of the cave. Of course, Plato does not believe, nor does his audience, that any such situation exists in fact; Platonists do not re-enact the story as a ritual; and there is little element of story at all—only an image.

With these preliminary distinctions, it is now possible to state a thesis about Tolkien's major works: they are an attempt to create literary myth that comes as close as is possible in our day to original myth. Tolkien was, of course, not foolish enough to think of himself as creating gospel (though a few of his madder readers may make this error). Tolkien gave his belief and allegiance to a particular gospel, Roman Catholic Christianity, and was in no danger of confusing what he was doing with *that.* Furthermore, Tolkien was *not* writing (and was indignant at any suggestion that he was writing) philosophical myth. His major works are not allegories, though one of his minor works, "Leaf by Niggle," *is* allegorical and is thus importantly different from the rest of his work.

In his essay "On Fairy Stories," Tolkien makes a distinction between primary belief, which is what believers in a gospel give to that gospel, and secondary belief, which we give to fiction. As Tolkien himself was well aware, the kind of belief that the pre-Christian world gave to original myth was somewhere in between primary and secondary belief; in fact, for convenience we will call it intermediate belief. In his essay on fairy stories, which are nowadays a form of literary myth, Tolkien was not directly concerned with original myth and did not need to discuss this point, though he mentions it indirectly.

It may be illuminating to apply our categories to something other than Tolkien at this point, and an example lies to hand: the Christian Gospels of Matthew, Mark, Luke, and John. Tolkien himself, his friend C. S. Lewis, and many other people in the modern world (myself included) regard the four Gospels as gospels in my technical sense and give them primary belief. At the other extreme, some "liberal" Christians appear to regard them as philosophical myths, embodying true ideas in the form of stories that have no literal truth at all.

But for our purposes, a more interesting attitude toward the four Gospels is that of the "liberal" Christian who is a "demythologizer." This person would feel about the four Gospels roughly what we said Homer and his audience felt about the Homeric stories. Matthew, Mark, Luke, and John are narratives in which legend, tradition, and history have been mixed with a good deal of human invention to produce a story that cannot and ought not command primary belief. The usual "demythologizer" wants to remove these "mythological accretions" and recover the historical facts underneath them (as suggested by the title of Albert Schweitzer's work *In Quest of the Historical Jesus*). More recently, some theologians have in various ways tried to suggest that we accept the four Gospels *as* original myth and, without trying to remove the mythical elements, give to these stories something like intermediate belief.

The motivation for this kind of suggestion is very often the realization that a person who accepts neither gospel nor original myth lives in an impoverished world, that there is a human need that was once satisfied by original myth and is still satisfied for many by gospel, a need that can be damaging to the human personality if it goes unfulfilled. Furthermore, neither philosophical myth nor literary myth is capable of completely filling this need, though they are often used in an attempt to satisfy it.

What is this need that gospel and original myth seem to fulfill whereas philosophical and literary myth do not? I think that it might be called the need for *significant form* in our experience. We want to be able to relate the things that happen to us as parts of an understandable whole. For some, the idea of Fate or the idea of the Will of God seems to satisfy this need, whereas for others, it is important that what happens be seen as due to their own choices, even choices made in a previous life, as in the myth or gospel (depending on your point of view) of karma or cosmic justice. What a myth or gospel does is to make such an abstract idea concrete by showing how significant form is exhibited in the events that occur to such awesome beings as gods or heroes or saints.

How does an original myth or gospel satisfy this need in a way in which a literary or philosophical myth does not? What does the job, I think, is the combination of Truth and Story. Literary myths have only story, with no truth, whereas philosophical myths may have truth but have discarded the vital melding of story with truth. A gospel given primary belief has an important advantage over an original myth that is not regarded as completely true and is only given intermediate belief.

Supposing, however, that someone is unwilling or unable to give primary belief to some gospel. Can this need then be satisfied by giving intermediate belief to some original myth? The difficulty is that you cannot simply *choose* to believe in any arbitrary story presented as original myth. Pre-Christian believers in original myth grew up in a general attitude of acceptance of the original myths of their culture. They could refuse to believe in these for any of a number of reasons, but they did not need to make a special effort, work themselves into a special frame of mind, to give intermediate belief to the original myths of their society.

People today are in a different situation. They face, on the one hand, the challenge of the Christian gospel, which claims complete truth and demands primary belief, and on the other hand, the challenge of science, which asks why anything that cannot be established by the methods of science should be given primary or even intermediate belief. A gospel may be able to meet this challenge, but a myth cannot. There is such a thing as apologetics: the reasoned defense of a religious belief or a gospel in my technical sense. But there is no such thing as apologetics for myth (though there are allegorical "explanations" of myth).

Now literary myth may embody a truth that is given primary belief: in Tolkien's *Silmarillion,* the world is created by God, an idea to which Tolkien gave primary belief. But Tolkien or his readers did not accept this idea because of Tolkien's literary myth. Rather, Tolkien wrote the myth, and some readers enjoy the myth, *because* of previously held beliefs. The belief creates the myth, not the myth the belief.

It follows from all this that anyone today who tried to create original myth would be facing an almost impossible task. However much the mythmaker wanted or intended to create original myth, there would be no real audience for it, and without an audience prepared to receive the myth, the communication would be incomplete. All that can be done in the modern world is to create literary myth that embodies truth believed independently of the myth. And this, I will argue, is just what Tolkien did.

As against this, we have some statements made by Tolkien himself that suggest that he saw himself in the role of a maker of original myth. In particular, there is a passage in a letter that has often been quoted by those writing about what Tolkien tried to achieve.

I was from early days grieved by the poverty of my own beloved country: it had no stories of its own (bound up with its tongue and style), not of the quality I sought, and found (as an ingredient) in legends of other lands. . . . I had a mind to make a body of more or less connected legend, ranging from the large and cosmogonic, to the level of romantic fairy story—the lesser in contact with the earth, the lesser drawing splendor from the vast backclothes —which I could dedicate simply: to England: to my country.[1]

However, it seems to me that this passage has been somewhat over-blown by some interpreters. Tolkien is speaking specifically of *stories,* to be enjoyed as stories, as fairy tales are. He says, indeed, that

myth and fairy-story must, as all art, reflect and contain in solution elements of moral and religious truth (or error) but not explicit, not in the known form of the primary "real" world (I am speaking, of course, of our present situation, not of ancient pagan, pre-Christian days).[2]

The key words in this passage, it seems to me, are "as all art." What Tolkien was writing was *literary* myth; he realized the absurdity in *post-*Christian days of attempting original myth.

Indeed, he might have learned this lesson from G. K. Chesterton, an author he mentions often and with respect. In his book *The Everlasting Man,* Chesterton insists on the basically artistic aspect of myth: myths are poetry and need a poet to criticize them. He points out that what I have called the need for significant form is best felt by the child or the artist.

Nobody understands it who has not felt what can only be called the ache of the artist to find some sense and some story in the beautiful things he sees: his hunger for secrets and his anger at any tree or town escaping with its tale untold. He feels that nothing is perfect unless it is personal.[3]

Indeed, Chesterton sees pre-Christian original myth as almost purely aesthetic in impulse.

The substance of all such paganism may be summarized thus. It is an attempt to reach the divine reality through the imagination alone: in its own field reason does not restrain it at all. . . . Mythology, then, sought God through imagination; or sought truth by means of beauty . . . but the imagination has its own laws and therefore its own triumphs which neither logicians or men of science can understand . . . mythology is a *search,* it is something that combines a recurrent desire with a recurrent doubt . . . the meaning of all the myths . . . is not the voice of the priest or a prophet saying "These things are." It is the voice of a dreamer and an idealist crying, "Why cannot these things be?"[4]

Chesterton draws together the symbols of demons, philosophers, and mythmakers in terms of characters in the story of Christ's nativity. Herod, who slaughtered the innocents, symbolizes the demons; the Three Wise Men symbolize the philosophers; and the shepherds symbolize the "men of the popular tradition who had everywhere been the makers of mythologies," in other words, the mythmakers. And Chesterton says of the cave or stable where Christ was born:

the place that the shepherds found was not an academy or an abstract republic; it was not a place of myths allegorized or dissected or explained away. It was a place of dreams come true. Since that hour no mythologies have been made in the world. Mythology is a search.[5]

This conclusion is one that Tolkien would neither want nor need to dispute: in the sense that mythology is a "search for the divine through imagination," Tolkien had no need or desire to create "a mythology for England." It was myth as story, myth as a form of artistic expression, that interested Tolkien; this was the gift he wished to give to his country, a literary, not a philosophical or religious, legacy.

This is not to say that there are not philosophical and religious ideas motivating Tolkien. As he says to one critic:

I would claim . . . to have as one object the elucidation of truth, and the encouragement of good morals in the real world by the ancient device of exemplifying them in unfamiliar embodiments, that may tend to "bring them home."[6]

And elsewhere Tolkien tells an inquirer:

The *Lord of the Rings* is, of course, a fundamentally religious and Catholic work, unconsciously so at first but consciously in the revision. That is why I have not put in anything like "religion" to cults or practices, in the imaginary world. For the religion is absorbed into the story and the symbolism.[7]

So far as the philosophical themes of the work, he says:

I do not think that even Power and Domination is the real center of my story. It provides the theme of a War, about something dark and threatening enough to seem at that time of supreme importance. But that is mainly "a setting" for the characters to show themselves. The real theme for me is about something much more permanent and difficult: Death and Immortality: the mystery of the love of the world in the hearts of a race "doomed" to leave and seemingly lose it: the anguish in the hearts of a race "doomed" not to leave it until its whole evil-aroused story is complete.[8]

Elsewhere he repeats the point.

The tale is not really about Power and Dominion: that only sets the wheels going: it is about Death and the desire for deathlessness. Which is hardly more than to say it is a tale written by a Man![9]

Note the capitalized "Man." The point is the same as in the previous quotation; the *human* problem is death and the desire for immortality, which Tolkien illuminates by "exemplifying them in unfamiliar embodiments"; the elvish problem is immortality and the desire for death.

Before we leave this general discussion of myth, it will be worthwhile to look at another view of myth by a close friend of Tolkien who was a perceptive critic and himself a creator of literary myth, C. S. Lewis. Chapter 5 of his book *An Experiment in Criticism* is entitled "On Myth." In this chapter Lewis admits he is using the word *myth* in a special and technical sense of his own.

> I must either use the word *myth* or coin a word and I think the former the lesser evil of the two. . . . A myth means, in this book, a story which has the following characteristics:
>
> 1. It is . . . extraliterary. . . .
> 2. The pleasure of myth depends hardly at all on such usual narrative attractions as suspense or surprise. Even at first hearing it is felt to be inevitable. And the first hearing is chiefly valuable in introducing us to a permanent object of contemplation—more like a thing than a narration—which works on us by its peculiar flavor or quality, rather as a smell or a chord does sometimes. Even from the first, there is hardly any narrative element. . . .
> 3. Human sympathy is at a minimum. We do not project ourselves at all strongly into the characters. They are like shapes moving in another world. We feel indeed that the pattern of their movements has a profound relevance to our own life, but we do not imaginatively transport ourselves into theirs. . . .
> 4. Myth is always in one sense of that word "fantastic." It deals with impossibles and preternaturals.
> 5. The experience may be sad or joyful but it is always grave. Comic myth (in my sense of *myth*) is impossible.
> 6. The experience is not only grave but awe-inspiring. We feel it to be numinous. It is as if something of great moment has been communicated to us. The recurrent efforts of the mind to grasp—we mean, chiefly, to conceptualize—this something is seen in the persistent tendency of humanity to provide myths with allegorical explanations. And after all allegories have been tried the myth itself continues to feel more important than they.[10]

By a myth in his sense being "extraliterary," Lewis means that the verbal account of the myth is not of primary importance.

> The man who first learns . . . a great myth through a verbal account which is badly or vulgarly or cacophonously written discounts and ignores the bad writing and attends solely to the myth. He hardly minds about the writing. He is glad to have the myth on any terms.[11]

Now obviously "myth" in Lewis's sense is not applicable to *The Lord of the Rings* or to *The Odyssey* or to some other forms of original myth. Even in some of the great Greek tragedies, there is suspense and human interest; even in some of the ceremonial re-enactments of myth there was room for humor. However, myth in Lewis's sense *is* to some extent characteristic of some of the background myths and legends in *The Lord of the Rings* and of a great deal of the *Silmarillion* and the *Unfinished Tales* of Tolkien. (In fact, Lewis mentions "the conception . . . of the Ents in Professor Tolkien's *Lord of the Rings*" as an example of myth in Lewis's sense.)

I think that Lewis defined an interesting category, something related to myth, that might be called the "numinous idea." Tolkien, like Lewis, had a taste for or attraction to such ideas, and his imagination was able to create such ideas as well as respond to them. But, for Tolkien, the "numinous idea" had to have certain specific characteristics. As he says in a letter to his son Christopher:

There are two quite different emotions: one that moves me supremely and I find small difficulty in evoking: the heart-racking sense of the vanished past (best expressed by Gandalf's words about the Palantír) and the other the more "ordinary" emotion, triumph, pathos, tragedy of the characters. That I am learning to do, as I get to know my people. But it is not really so near my heart and is forced on me by the fundamentally literary dilemma. A story must be told or there is no story, but it is the untold stories that are the most moving.[12]

The point I want to emphasize here is that it is the *past*, the unknown, unrecorded past that is numinous for Tolkien. A Lewisian myth could in principle be about the future: perhaps even Lewis (who disliked Wells) might admit that certain parts of H. G. Wells's "The Time Machine" approach the dignity of myth. Wells gives an image of the end of the human race that remains in the mind as "an object of contemplation." But granted that it is the *past* that especially arouses the feeling of the numinous in Tolkien, we can see that some of what Tolkien did was an effort to evoke numinous ideas: myths in Lewis's sense.

For example, Tolkien was haunted by an image of the destruction of Atlantis: a great wave sweeping over a green and civilized land. Some of his earliest writings attempted to embody this image in poetry or story. But in some sense it was the evocation, even the exorcism from his dreams, of this image that he was trying to attain, rather than the telling of an enjoyable story. When he wrote *The Lord of the Rings,* however, he realized, as our earlier quotation shows, that he had to introduce suspense, characterization, even humor.

How, then, does *The Lord of the Rings,* and even *The Hobbit,* "approach the dignity of myth," as I said earlier? In some ways very much as Homer does. In the *Iliad,* Homer does not attempt to recount the whole history of the Trojan War, he takes a short period near the end of the war and lets all that has gone before and all that is to follow appear indirectly in the story he does tell—that of the wrath of Achilles and its effect on the war.

As E. V. Rieu says in the preface to his translation of the *Iliad,* "The action of the Iliad covers only fifty days in a ten years' war. But . . . Homer causes two shadows to add their somber significance to every page, that of the past and that of what is still to come."[13]

Now Homer could rely on his audience knowing and even believing in great part the stories about the earlier and later events of the war; thus he could evoke intermediate belief for his telling of the story. Tolkien's initial audience had no idea at all of the vast and involved legends that Tolkien had evolved over the years and, of course, no belief in them. So when Tolkien wrote of "The Shadow of the Past" he had to *present* the past events in some fashion as well as show their effect on the events of his narrative.

Furthermore, though Homer pictures his gods with very "human" failings, and even uses a great deal of humor in his description of them, Rieu notes that

what is so remarkable is the fact that Homer leaves us with the feeling not only that he believes in his gods but that they were indeed very worshipful and formidable powers. Moreover the Greeks accepted him as their first theologian and creator of the Olympian religion.[14]

That is an achievement possible only where an "aesthetic" religion, as described by Chesterton, is still possible, where there is an audience who will accept a religion because of its beauty. Tolkien, who has to *create* belief in his legends (but only secondary, literary belief), is not so free to season them with humor. There is not much use of humor in connection with the "numinous" characters in Tolkien, such as the Elves, but there is some. Tom Bombadil, for example, is a character who is both numinous and humorous. However, the kind of humor that is impossible in myth is the kind that mocks at or questions the basis of the myth itself. As Rieu notes:

The comic element is introduced almost solely on occasions when gods are *shown together* in sympathetic or hostile action. When dealing with mankind, each in his own capacity, they are far from amusing. . . . Homer therefore reveres his gods but rightly feels that it would be untrue to life to make these formidable creatures take one another as seriously as *he* takes each of them . . . but the gods do not retaliate by laughing at mankind . . . they take men seriously and regard them as miserable though fascinating creatures.[15]

The problem for the creator of literary myth in the modern age, when the objects of primary religious belief have so often been scoffed at, is to create gods and heroes who can be taken seriously, can be given even secondary belief. To do this the author must take them seriously, and the characters in the story must take them seriously. Even a hint of a snigger behind the hand, of an attitude of "we can't *really* take this seriously, but let's pretend," is fatal to secondary belief. That is precisely what makes so many modern fantasies ultimately unsatisfactory: we cannot take them seriously because their authors do not. And it seems to be the case that those who have a real primary belief in persons or things that they believe to be real and numinous, as Tolkien and C. S. Lewis did, have the best chance of producing stories in which fictional numinous persons or objects can command secondary belief.

This is not surprising when we reflect that the artist must draw on his or her experience. Those with an experience of really having been in love can write convincing stories of love; those who really believe in a real God and revere real saints can write convincingly of gods and heroes. In many modern writers, the instinct for reverence, for awe, seems dead—or at least weak from disuse.

There are also various literary devices, which can to some extent be taught or learned by trial and error, for writing convincingly of numinous persons or objects. It is far more effective to describe them indirectly by their effect on persons and things in the story than to describe them directly. They must be brought "on stage" sparingly but never entirely forgotten. In Tolkien we recognize the sinister power of the Ring by its *effect* on Bilbo, on Gollum, on Sam, and especially on Frodo, more than by anything that is said directly about it. Tolkien has been criticized for making Sauron, his chief representative of evil, only a brooding presence in the background, but this is far more effective than any amount of direct description that might attempt to arouse feelings of horror.

Also, numinous persons or objects must be presented with a certain amount of dignity, both in action and in speech. This is very difficult to do if they are shown doing ordinary things such as sleeping or eating or if they are pictured as speaking colloquially. It is almost impossible if they are shown doing actions we feel to be undignified or pictured as speaking slang. (The balance between too little dignity and too much is hard to strike. When in a fantasy of my own I found it necessary to bring the god Apollo on stage and have him speak to a young woman from modern times, one sympathetic critic said that I had made him talk as if he were addressing a public meeting, and another said that the first critic "just didn't know how a god should talk.")

To conclude this chapter, let us take the first of several looks at Tolkien's almost too well known essay "On Fairy Stories." I say almost too well known because the more obvious points Tolkien makes in this essay have been repeated over and over again, and the subtler points have often been neglected. One such point is the relation between fairy stories and myth. For Tolkien they are a continuum: fairy stories are merely "lower mythology," the part of mythology that is humbler and closer to the earth.

He considers and rejects the view that mythology is simply an allegorization of natural forces and the view that folk and fairy tales are a sort of debased or worn-down mythology. Whether we take this view that there are real persons and things that myth and folktale speak of or the view that the myths and fairy stories are only the product of human imagination, "There is no fundamental distinction between the higher and the lower mythologies."[16]

This means that we can take a good deal of what Tolkien says about fairy stories as applying to myth. If we do this, we can see certain important contrasts between Tolkien's view of myth and Lewis's. For Tolkien, myth does not exclude humor: "There is satire, sustained or intermittent, in undoubted fairy-stories, and satire may often have been intended in traditional tales where we do not now perceive it."[17] However, Tolkien notes, "If there is any satire present in the tale, one thing must not be made fun of, the magic itself."[18]

Since Tolkien is speaking of fairy tales as *stories* enjoyed today, that is, as literary myths in our sense, he does not, as we noted earlier, need to make a distinction between the sort of belief we give to a powerful story when caught up in its spell and the sort of belief an ancient Greek might have given to the myths about the gods. But some of the things he says about secondary belief could be applied to myth as well as to story. He quarrels with the formula "willing suspension of disbelief" for the kind of belief we give to works of literary art, because it suggests something self-consciously insincere, some deliberate element of "let's pretend." Rather, he says, a good story casts a spell on us, convinces us temporarily of the imaginary world of the story, which has its own standards of truth.

For this reason he rejects stories set in a dream-frame as having any possible relation to fairy tale and myth, for

since the fairy story deals with "marvels" it cannot tolerate any frame or machinery suggesting that the whole story in which they occur is a figment or illusion . . . if a waking writer tells you that his tale is only a thing imagined in his sleep he cheats deliberately the primal desire at the heart of Faerie: the realization, independent of the conceiving mind, of imagined wonder.[19]

This recalls Chesterton's thesis about the essentially aesthetic nature of original myth: that it represented "the voice of the dreamer and idealist crying, 'why cannot these things be?'."

The "primal desire" that Tolkien speaks of with regard to fairy tales is considerably constrained in the modern reader by religion or lack of religion and by the challenge of science. But for the ancient Greek (to take only one example of a pre-Christian pagan), neither gospel nor science restrained the "will to believe," and the "spell" cast by myths and marvelous stories may well have led to a stronger, more or less permanent state of something like what Tolkien calls secondary belief; this is precisely what I earlier called intermediate belief.

To create secondary belief in the reader of a modern tale of marvels, there must be no break in the mood, no laughing at the magic, no metaphorical nudging of the reader in the ribs. This seriousness about the work must be in the writer before it can be in the reader, and it is one reason why Tolkien speaks of his stories as if they were discovered rather than invented, one reason why in lecturing to a university audience on fairy stories he deliberately speaks as if it were an open question whether the Elves and the realm of Faerie exist in reality.

But nothing would be further from Tolkien's intention than for any of his readers to give primary or even intermediate belief to Tolkien's imagined world and characters. That would be to confuse literary myth with original myth or myth with gospel. And though in Tolkien's view the Christian gospel does satisfy certain intense longings in the human personality, it should not be accepted *because* it satisfies those longings: rather, it can really satisfy those longings only because it is true.

There is no tale ever told that men would rather find true, and none which so many skeptical men have accepted as true on its own merits. For the Art of it has the supremely convincing tone of Primary Art, that is, of Creation. To reject it leads either to sadness or to wrath. . . . This story is supreme and it is true. Art has been verified.

God is the lord of angels and of men—and of elves. Legend and History have met and fused.[20]

2. Three Faces of Myth

Since we have established that Tolkien thought of myth and fairy tale as on a continuum, we can make use of a good many points in Tolkien's essay "On Fairy Stories" to further our understanding of how Tolkien regarded myth. And we can increase our understanding of the essay "On Fairy Stories" by looking at the short story, "Leaf by Niggle," that Tolkien chose to publish along with the essay in a book titled *Tree and Leaf.*

It is always tempting to read too much meaning into historical accidents, and no doubt it is partly a historical accident that "Leaf by Niggle" was the story chosen by Tolkien to make, along with his previously written and published essay "On Fairy Stories," the content of the book *Tree and Leaf* published in 1965. Still, Tolkien explicitly tells us in the "Introductory Note" to *Tree and Leaf* that they were "written in the same period (1938–39)" and that "they are related: by the symbols of Tree and Leaf and by both touching in different ways on what is called in the essay 'sub-creation.'" The unexpectedness of the choice of "Leaf by Niggle" to accompany "On Fairy Stories" arises from the difference between it and most of Tolkien's other fiction. Some differences are obvious, others less obvious. First, "Leaf by Niggle" is allegorical. Second, it makes no mention of Elves or the land of Faerie. Third, in it a religious element is explicit rather than implicit.

Each of these differences from Tolkien's other work is surprising—so surprising, in fact, that I will have to argue presently that they actually exist and are not figments of my imagination. Cumulatively, they raise the question of why so untypical a work should have been chosen to accompany and illustrate "On Fairy Stories." What I am going to claim, and try to argue for, is that Tolkien deliberately chose to make explicit in "Leaf by Niggle" some things that are implicit in all of his work; that "Leaf by Niggle" was chosen for *Tree and Leaf* because it is midway between the essay "On Fairy Stories," in which

Tolkien talks about his work, and most of the other fiction and poetry, in which he simply gets on with it. To argue these claims, I will confine myself to *Tree and Leaf* itself and to Tolkien's other "minor" works, leaving till later the application of what I say to *The Hobbit* and to *The Lord of the Rings*. The things I will be talking about are just as much in *The Hobbit* and the trilogy as in the "minor" works, but the richness and complexity of the major works makes these things less visible.

I will begin with the first, and perhaps most controversial, claim I have made: that "Leaf by Niggle" is allegorical. Does not Tolkien explicitly say in the preface to the Ballantine edition of *The Lord of the Rings* that "I cordially dislike allegory in all its manifestations"? He does indeed, but there I think he exaggerates. He is reacting against the idea that *The Lord of the Rings* is an allegory—which, of course, it is not—and he is also taking "allegory" very strictly. As he says, "many confuse 'applicability' with 'allegory,' but the one resides in the freedom of the reader and the other in the proposed domination of the author."[1] We see, then, that when he thinks of allegory, he is thinking of philosophy or fiction dressed up as story, in which each person and event "stands for" some idea or some fact of the real world (what I would call strict allegory).

"Leaf by Niggle" is not an allegory in that sense, and I would not object to rephrasing my claim by saying that "Leaf by Niggle" is *applicable* rather than *allegorical*. But applicable it certainly is, and it is intended to be not just in one way but in at least three. The "freedom of the reader," as I think Tolkien would agree, is never absolute: to "apply" a work clean against the intentions of the author is an intellectual sin, comparable to misrepresenting a person's statement or character. But in "Leaf by Niggle" there are at least three applications that "come to mind," come to our minds because they came to Tolkien's first.

The first application is what might be called the "moral" application and can if you choose be made entirely this-worldly. To contrast it more clearly with another application to be considered later, I will interpret it this way. On this interpretation, then, Niggle is Everyman, and the application is to a person's work and to the individual's relation to others and to society. The theme of the work, so interpreted, is that morally speaking our relations to other human beings come before, are morally more important than, our careers, our life work, our "projects" for ourselves and for our lives, and that society insofar as it embodies the demand that we heed this order of priorities is just and makes legitimate demands on us. But if society goes beyond these just demands and tries to make us subordinate to social forms, it is unjust and detestable. Furthermore, says the story, the conflict between career and personal relations is often, though not always, illusory: it is our weaknesses and failings that lead us to situations in which we must neglect one obligation to fulfill another, and if we give due place to personal relations, it will be the better for our careers as ourselves. However, though this represents the moral ideal, we all fail to live up to it and need to have strict justice "tempered with mercy."

In the story, Niggle's attempts to finish his last work, a great picture of a tree, is interfered with by visiting friends, by Parish, a demanding neighbor, and by Inspectors who require that he fulfill civic duties. Niggle's picture, of course, represents his career, his lifework, his "project." The laws, the Inspectors, represent the legitimate demands of the moral law. These are stern, they are "awe-full" in the true sense of inspiring awe; but they are not intended to be hateful or villainous, and anyone who sees them as such is seriously misunderstanding Tolkien's intention. Notice that Niggle's conscience is in full agreement with the demand of the laws; he knows what he ought to do and feels guilty when he does not do it. The moral duties that Tolkien chooses as examples of conflict between duties to others and one's career or job are simple and straightforward ones. The visitors who interrupt Niggle's work in the summer are a nuisance, but "he could not deny that he had invited them himself, away back in the winter, when he had not thought it an 'interruption' to visit the shops and have tea with his acquaintances in the town." Repaying favors others have done you, carrying out commitments you have voluntarily made, these are very basic parts of morality.

Another thing we see in this quotation is that Niggle has brought some of his troubles on himself. If he had worked in the winter when he could work without interruption, he would not be working against time now. Some of Niggle's "interruptions" come from sources beyond his control: the weather and Parish and Parish's wife. But, again, if Niggle had done what he could when he could, he would have been ready for such demands. "One thing he kept repeating to himself ... 'I wish I had called on Parish the first morning when the high winds began. I meant to. The first loose tiles would have been easy to fix. Then Mrs. Parish might never have caught cold. Then I should not have caught cold either. Then I should have had a week longer.' "

After Niggle is forced to take the journey, we have the might-have-been, the ideal. If Niggle had learned before his journey the lessons he is forced to learn in the "workhouse," he could have handled his problems better; after the workhouse he began to be "master of his time; he began to know just what he could do with it. There was no sense of rush. He was quieter inside now, and at resting time he could really rest." Furthermore, if he had reached out to Parish before the journey as he does after, Parish would not have been just a nuisance and an interruption. He could have remembered before his journey that Parish "was a very good neighbor and let me have excellent potatoes very cheap which saved me a lot of time." He could have reflected then that "Parish's leg gave him a wretched time." If he had thought of Parish as a person and not an interruption, he could have shared then in Parish's knowledge of the soil and growing things, and Parish might have responded, if only out of courtesy, by trying to really look at Niggle's painting. Parish then was not a person to Niggle, because Niggle did not think of him as a person but as an interruption.

But Tolkien's message is not simple optimism, good in everything and everyone. Councillor Tompkins represents a deeper rejection of personality, thinking of Niggle as "worthless," as someone who "could have been made into a serviceable cog of some sort ... washing dishes in a communal kitchen or something." Tompkins talks of Society, but we find that some, at least, of his motives are self-interested; he covets Niggle's house. The inspectors, the driver, the First Voice are not meant to be hateful or to be villains, but Tompkins is, a minor villain but a villain nevertheless, "capable of a little evil in a mean sort of way."

On this interpretation we need not think of the journey as death, only as the gap between the actual and the ideal, which we are obliged to try to close. Things could be as they are after the journey; they are more likely to be as they are before it, so we all need mercy, we all need the Second Voice to plead in our favor. In turn, as we expect mercy, we should be merciful to others: the Second Voice excuses Niggle to the First Voice, but Niggle excuses Parish to the First Voice also. Justice, mercy, duty, kindness—all this is moral yet not religious, and it is a true "application" of Niggle's story.

But there are at least two others. The second I will call the "aesthetic" application of "Leaf by Niggle." On this interpretation, Niggle is not Everyman but "Every artist." His picture is not just *a* career but a dedication to Art, to any one of the arts. The major theme on this interpretation is the relation of the artist to his or her art and to society. The world before the journey is again the real, the world after the journey the ideal; Tompkins again represents the wrong view of things. But the interpretation of some details changes, and details previously left out assume new importance.

The major question now becomes whether the artist should sacrifice personal relations to his or her art. In the early part of the story the dilemma is posed; we all have some tendency to sympathize with Niggle and feel that he should send away the visitors, slam the door on Parish, and complete his picture. The whole romantic tradition about the artist tells us that this is the right answer; art comes before personal obligations; Gauguin is right to leave his family and go to Tahiti to paint. William Faulkner once expressed this point of view: "If a writer has to rob his mother he will not hesitate: the 'Ode to a Grecian Urn' is worth any number of old ladies."

But this is not Tolkien's answer. As the world after the journey shows us, Niggle's problems arose partly from his not being master of his time or fully master of his craft. The problem did not come essentially from the demands others made on him but rather from Niggle's own weaknesses. The right personal relationships would have strengthened his art, not weakened it; here again Parish is the symbol at first of the wrong relationship to others and after the journey of the right relationship: Niggle's picture without Parish's contribution would not be as good a *picture*.

Councillor Tompkins's attitude toward art is doubly wrong. First he dismisses beauty as a subjective delusion; Niggle was "always fiddling with leaves and flowers. I asked him why once. He said he thought they were pretty. Can you believe it? He said *pretty!* 'What, digestive and genital organs of plants?' I said to him; and he had nothing to answer. Silly footler!" But as the Shepherd has told Parish just previously, Niggle's picture, and all art, is an effort to convey a vision of something more real, more true, than the world of sense.

Tompkins's second error is that the only importance of art is its political value. He says of Niggle, "You couldn't make use of his painting. There's plenty of scope for bold young men not afraid of new ideas and new methods. None of this old-fashioned stuff. Private day-dreaming. He could not have designed a telling poster to save his life." But this, according to Tolkien, is an error about the political realm, which should serve and enhance the personal, and also about the role of art, which is valuable in itself and in its contribution to personal life. As Niggle says earlier, "It's a gift."

In fact, one artist to whom this application of "Leaf by Niggle" is especially appropriate is Tolkien himself. As he says in a letter to an inquirer:

"Leaf by Niggle" arose suddenly and almost complete. It was written down almost at a sitting and very nearly in the form in which it now appears. Looking at it now from a distance I should say that, in addition to my tree-love (it was originally called *The Tree*), it arose from my own preoccupation with *The Lord of the Rings,* the knowledge that it would be finished in great detail or not at all, and the fear (near certainty) that it would be "not at all." The war had arisen to darken all horizons. But no such analyses are a complete explanation even of a short story.[2]

"Leaf by Niggle" was published in 1945, but if we accept Tolkien's statement that it was written during the period "1938–39," this would put it in the early days of England's involvement in World War II. Reference to his letters at this time show that Tolkien was working on various possible successors to *The Hobbit,* primarily what became *The Lord of the Rings,* but he was also writing and illustrating a children's story called "Mr. Bliss" (not published until 1982) and was retyping and reworking *Farmer Giles of Ham.* He was having health and domestic problems and working at grading examination papers from other universities to make money for his family. In addition, he was working on various scholarly projects, including an introduction to a translation of *Beowulf.* No doubt there were other personal demands on him that do not appear in the published letters. So Tolkien had good reason to feel as distracted and pulled in all directions as Niggle himself.

Third, I want to touch on the religious application of "Leaf by Niggle." In this interpretation Niggle is again Everyman, but now for the first time the journey has its in some ways obvious interpretation: it is death. The picture is again one's career or lifework or "project," and the calls on Niggle's time are again the demands of morality. But the kaleidoscope has shifted again, and new elements come into prominence. The message of the story up to the journey is that both our lifework and our personal relations are unsatisfactory and fragmentary; we succeed at neither because of our own laziness, timidity, and general inadequacy. But the message of the second part of the story is the joyous one that nothing is wasted. What seems to be our failure at our lifework will blossom into success; what seem to be our failures in personal relations will also be redeemed.

In Shakespeare's *As You Like It* there is a lovely line (tossed off by a minor character in a minor scene, like so many of Shakespeare's best lines), "Hereafter in a better world than this I will desire more love and knowledge of you." This is what we all desire, or ought to desire, of those we have loved so inadequately, of those we have failed to love, though we had the chance. Tolkien shows this "better love and knowledge" in the case of Niggle and Parish; he hints at it in the case of Parish and his wife. As before, we must not jump to an easy optimism. There is good in everyone, true enough, but in this life that goodness is soured and spoiled by our obstinate refusal to be what we could be. Parish before the journey is really a boor, his wife really a shrew. As the Shepherd tells Parish, he could and should have tried harder about Niggle's picture and about other things.

Tolkien does not promise "cheap grace" or easy salvation; we see the difficulty of Niggle's re-formation and have hints of it in Parish's case. Parish needs Niggle's help; his wife will need his. Growing into what we should be is not an easy process or one we can carry out without the help of our friends. Tolkien's fellow Catholics can find here a new version of the traditional doctrine of purgatory; adherents of other religious traditions will interpret this in their own way. But in terms of human relationships, what we have lost or thrown away can and will be regained, Tolkien tells us here.

Not only our life but also our work, our careers, our projects for life will be redeemed if there is anything in them that can be redeemed. Parish the farmer finds a new depth in his love for the soil and growing things; Niggle the artist finds new meaning in and new use for his artistic vision. And just as Niggle's art can affect Parish as it never did in life, so Parish's skill with nature can help Niggle as it never could in life. Somehow in ways we cannot guess the salesman's desire to "work with people," the actress's desire to entertain and be admired, will bear fruit in their own lives and the lives of others.

As in our other interpretations, Councillor Tompkins provides the counterpoint. For him there is no life after death. The journey is "a meaningless old expression," and to die is to "go though the tunnel into the great Rubbish Heap." For a man who thinks like this, it is understandable that society is more important than the individual, that art is either "private daydreaming" or something to be used politically. Tompkins lives in a world without any transcendent values; in such a world perhaps it makes sense to grab what you can: political power— or Niggle's cottage.

The last scene is counterpoint in another sense, too; success in heavenly terms is not success in worldly terms. Niggle in the land beyond the journey is a complete success. His earthly life has been fulfilled, and he is ready to journey into the mountains, which are Tolkien's metaphor for "exploration into God." As he says to Parish, "Things could have been different, but they could not have been better." But Niggle in this world, the world before the journey, is forgotten, insignificant, a failure, forgotten except for a lingering fragment, one leaf, of his destroyed work.

There is nothing in Tolkien's published letters that strongly supports the religious interpretation, but in one letter he does say that

in my myth I have used "subcreation" in a special way (not the same as "subcreation" as a term in criticism of art, though I tried to show allegorically how that might come to be taken up into creation in my "purgatorial" story "Leaf by Niggle").[3]

By calling "Leaf by Niggle" a purgatorial story, Tolkien indirectly refers to the Catholic idea of purgatory, and it is interesting that he specifically says that he makes a certain point "allegorically." In another letter, however, he says that he prefers to call "Leaf by Niggle" mythical rather than allegorical, on the grounds that "Niggle is meant to be a real mixed quality *person* and not an 'allegory' of any single vice or virtue."[4] But this is a very narrow interpretation of allegory: not all allegories feature personified vices and virtues.

We have three interpretations, then, of a seemingly simple story. Are there more? Perhaps, but as W. H. Auden reminds us, "Though a work of literature can be read in a number of ways, this number is finite and can be arranged in a hierarchical order; some readings are obviously 'truer' than others, some doubtful, some obviously false, and some . . . absurd."[5] The three "readings" I have given of "Leaf by Niggle" are, I believe, the primary ones, the ones intended by Tolkien. The very fact that each interpretation fits in negatively with one element of Tompkins's attitudes gives us some indication that we are on the right track.

The second claim of the three I began with is obvious enough in one way: that there is no mention of Elves or of the land of Faerie in "Leaf by Niggle." But although obvious, it is also surprising, for in "On Fairy Stories" Tolkien *defines* a fairy story as one having to do with the "Perilous Realm," the land of Faerie, or with its inhabitants. Why then choose a story, "Leaf by Niggle," that has no trace of Faerie or its inhabitants to companion the essay "On Fairy Stories"?

Once we see this anomaly, it is so surprising that we may be tempted to try to explain it away. After all, we might say, is not the land beyond the journey, especially after Niggle leaves the workhouse, a sort of land of Faerie, magical and beautiful? But I think that Tolkien himself would very strongly reject this idea. The country beyond the journey, as we have seen, can be taken as a metaphor, an analogy for an ideal state of morality or art, or for an image of heaven. It is, moreover, interpreted as a paradise, a good place, intended for human beings of our world—Niggle, Parish, Parish's wife. None of this is at all true of Faerie. That Perilous Realm is a place in its own right, not a metaphor or analogy for anything else. And Tolkien says emphatically that "the road to fairyland is not the road to Heaven."[6] Furthermore, it is not a place intended for, or even hospitable to, human beings, except for a favored few. It and its inhabitants are separated from human beings and their history; "Elves are not primarily concerned with us or we with them. Our fates are sundered and our paths seldom meet." So the land beyond the journey is not Faerie; it may be *a* perilous realm, but it is not *that* Perilous Realm.

My third point, that "Leaf by Niggle" is *explicitly* religious, unlike the rest of Tolkien's fiction, must be understood in terms of Tolkien's character. He was a reticent man, and what is explicit for him is, compared with his friend C. S. Lewis, for example, very unexplicit. But although I began with the moral and aesthetic applications of "Leaf by Niggle," I think that it is clear that the religious interpretation is the deepest and the most adequate. The very fact that it can be given a religious interpretation at all makes it unique among Tolkien's work; there is no plausible religious interpretation of, for example, "Smith of Wooton Major" or *The Hobbit.* Only at the end of the trilogy, where Frodo's journey deepens into a Way of the Cross, does a religious element become explicit in any other work of Tolkien.

I hope that I have established my three points—that "Leaf by Niggle" is allegorical, not about Faerie or Elves, and explicitly (for Tolkien) religious—at least well enough to serve as a basis for further discussion. The question now becomes, Why did Tolkien choose this to go with "On Fairy Stories" to make the book *Tree and Leaf?* I do not discount accident; perhaps this was the only finished piece he had to hand when his publishers clamored for "a new Tolkien book" after the astonishing success of *The Lord of the Rings.* But Tolkien's professional conscience would not have let him put just anything together in a book, and in fact, I will argue that there is a real unity in *Tree and Leaf.*

The major link is just where Tolkien tells us to look—in that "On Fairy Stories" helps us to see what aspect of subcreation "Leaf by Niggle" illuminates. The passage comes, significantly, in a part of the essay where Tolkien mentions George MacDonald.

Something really "higher" is occasionally glimpsed in mythology: Divinity, the right to power (as distinct from its possession), the due of worship; in fact "religion" . . . mythology and religion are two distinct things that have become inextricably tangled . . . or maybe they were sundered long ago and have since groped slowly through a labyrinth of error through confusion, back towards re-fusion. Even fairy-stories as a whole have three faces: the Mystical towards the supernatural; the Magical towards Nature; and the Mirror of scorn and pity towards Man. The essential face of Faerie is the middle one, the Magical. But the degree in which the others appear (if at all) is variable and may be decided by the individual story teller. The Magical, the fairy-story, may . . . be made a vehicle for Mystery. This at least is what George MacDonald attempted, achieving stories of power and beauty when he succeeded, as in *The Golden Key* (which he called a fairy-tale).[7]

This passage gives us the essential clue to understanding Tolkien's minor works of fiction. "Leaf by Niggle" shows us the mystical face of fairy story; *Farmer Giles of Ham* shows us the mirror of Man, pity and scorn masked by laughter but still there as in all comedy with any depth. *Smith of Wooton Major* gives us the central, magical face of fairy tale. Neither *Farmer Giles of Ham* nor *Smith of Wooton Major* is allegorical; neither has any religious element. Farmer Giles lives in a mythical Merry England with that magical beast the Dragon at large; Smith lives on the borders of Faerie and is made free of it by its King and Queen.

The term Tolkien himself preferred for "Leaf by Niggle" is *myth*. It is a philosophical myth in the Platonic sense, the presentation in the form of a story of a deep truth. It meets some of the conditions given by C. S. Lewis in *An Experiment in Criticism*, "a particular kind of story which has a value in itself . . . we feel it to be numinous. It is as if something of great moment had been communicated to us."

Tolkien is using fairy story as MacDonald did and as C. S. Lewis did in the Narnia stories, to embody religious belief. The part of "On Fairy Stories" that is in a way most relevant to "Leaf by Niggle" is that "concluding unscientific postscript" in which Tolkien for once speaks explicitly and directly of the religious belief that was so deep a part of his nature. The gospel story is the greatest of myths, but in C. S. Lewis's phrase, it is "myth become fact." The story of our redemption, Tolkien tells us in "On Fairy Stories," is the greatest of all myths but greater still because it is true. In "Leaf by Niggle" he gives us a new myth embodying part of that truth.

In the body of "On Fairy Stories" Tolkien tells us that artistic creation is *subcreation,* making in one sense "a world of our own." But in the epilogue he tells us, "Probably every writer making a secondary world . . . hopes that he is drawing on reality, hopes that the peculiar quality of this secondary world (if not all the details) are derived from Reality or are flowing into it." This derivation from or flowing into the real world can be found in all of Tolkien's work: in its moral soundness and seriousness, in its artistic integrity, and in its underlying religious framework, made explicit only occasionally but always there.

3. Myth and Story

Though Tolkien's work has, as we have seen, a deep affinity with traditional myth, it is "packaged" and "marketed" as fantasy or even science fiction. Yet the market for Tolkien's work is far wider than the market for other kinds of fantasy or science fiction: evidently some readers have a taste for Tolkien that does not extend to other writers who seem superficially similar to him. We can gain a better understanding of both Tolkien and myth if we examine the nature of fantasy and science fiction, how Tolkien's work is like and unlike other work in these genres, and how fantasy and science fiction are related to myth.

Historically it might be argued that science fiction is a subdivision of the older and broader category of fantasy. But in terms of recent history, fantasy as a publishing category grew out of science fiction and still has close ties with it. Modern science fiction is usually thought of as having its origins in the 1920s when an editor named Hugo Gernsbeck began a magazine that featured stories about the future and the marvelous scientific discoveries and inventions that might shape it. Appropriately, the magazine was named *Amazing Stories*.

At first *Amazing Stories* and its imitators seemed to be only another ripple in the flood of magazine fiction printed on cheap pulp paper with garish and colorful covers—generically, pulp magazines, or "pulps." These magazines were a major source of entertainment in pre-television America, and appealed to much the same audience as television does today. There were romance "pulps," pulps for mysteries, spy stories, war stories, Westerns, and even more specialized categories, such as sea stories or "air war" stories.

But gradually science fiction pulps began to distinguish themselves from other pulp magazines. Their readers were far more intelligent and well educated than the average pulp reader and showed a tendency to form groups and clubs to discuss and promote their favorite form of reading. Gradually the quality of stories rose, and stories began to exhibit genuine scientific knowledge as well as a "sense of wonder" that went far beyond the naive awe at the wonders of science characteristic of the early science fiction magazines.

Very little real science fiction was appearing in book form at this time. H. G. Wells in England was publishing occasional novels and short stories that were genuine science fiction. The stories of Jules Verne were still popular, and a few other writers, such as Olaf Stapledon, were struggling to express their ideas in this form. But by and large, modern science fiction was a magazine phenomenon, and writers like Robert Heinlein and Isaac Asimov who are bestselling authors today learned their trade writing for the early science fiction pulps.

What is science fiction? Giving a definition of anything so complex is difficult. The trouble is that any simple definition will have too many exceptions, and any definition without exceptions will be as complex as a legal contract. The reason for the complexity is the same in both cases—the need to close up all the loopholes and take care of all the borderline cases. Rather than a formal definition, I will give a set of overlapping criteria for what makes a story science fiction. If it has many of these characteristics or has any of them to an outstanding degree, a story, whether it is written or told or filmed or performed live or on television, will be what is ordinarily called science fiction, whether those who create or present it want to call it that or not.

A story, then, is science fiction if

it is about the future; *or*

it involves space travel of a kind that has not occurred at the time the story is created; *or*

it involves events taking place on a planet or location other than Earth, but in our universe, or else in an alternative universe; *or*

it involves telepathy or other "psi" phenomena; *or*

it involves nonhuman persons or subpersonal creatures that do not exist in the real world but are not "supernatural" (I will call these "alien" persons or creatures); *or*

it involves an imaginary scientific discovery or a mechanical device of a kind that does not exist at the time of writing and may never exist (I will call these "fantastic" discoveries or machines).

A story that has all or most of these characteristics will be a "paradigm case," or standard example, of science fiction.

Stories that involve only one of the seven elements may be clearly science fiction or on the borderline, depending on the degree to which the element is present. Ordinary fiction may be set slightly in the future for a variety of reasons (perhaps the author wants to describe a political situation, a stock market manipulation, a threat of war, etc. that has never really occurred). That does not in itself make the story science fiction. Similarly, a story could involve space exploration techniques only slightly advanced over present ones and use them as the basis for a spy story or a realistic novel of industrial intrigue: the science fiction element would be too slight to make the work science fiction. James Bond movies are often described as having "science fiction gadgets" but are not thought of as *being* science fiction. Scientific discoveries or marvelous machines can be used peripherally in a realistic novel; for example, a psychological novel about the career pressures of a doctor might involve a startling new medical discovery. Telepathy or other psi phenomena may be used as minor elements in a gothic novel or a detective story without making the story as a whole science fiction. Off-Earth locations, time travel, and genuinely alien persons or creatures are harder to assimilate into realistic fiction, but when such elements are outweighed by treatment and other plot elements characteristic of "mainstream" fiction, we hesitate to label the result science fiction.

On the other hand, even one science fiction element, if it is important enough to the story, can make us think of the work as a whole as science fiction. A good test is to ask what the book as a whole is "about." If it is reasonable to say that the book is "about" space travel, time travel, telepathy, and so on (even though it may be "about" other things too, such as courage, sexual equality, or religion), then it seems reasonable to call the work science fiction.

This raises two questions: what part must *science* play in science fiction, and what part must *ideas* play in science fiction, as opposed to, say, adventure or character. First, the part that science must play: you can insist that a science fiction story contain scientific elements that are extrapolated from or at least compatible with present-day scientific knowledge; if you do, you are not defining science fiction as it is ordinarily understood but *re*defining it in a narrower way.

The fact is that, if science appears at all, in much science fiction it appears as a *means*. As we all know, science has already enabled us to travel in space and may enable us to travel much farther and faster. The only locations for human activity that we know to exist are other planets of our own star and other stars, and our only realistic hope of reaching them is by the further development of science and technology. Time travel is quite likely not possible, but if it were, only science offers much hope of attaining it. If telepathy and other psi phenomena are fact, we count on science to discover it, and if they can be further developed, science seems to offer the best hope of doing so. Any alien persons or animals that exist are most likely to be discovered by science, and if none exist, science is most likely to create them. Marvelous discoveries or mechanisms are something science has given us in the past and is sure to give us again. The future, of course, will not be brought about by science, but in all likelihood science will have a great effect on the shape it takes. But science fiction today is interested mostly in the end results brought about by means of science, not in the means by which they are brought about. It would be possible, though very difficult, to write about the process by which science discovers truth and technology brings about changes, but the average science fiction story assumes that the process has been completed. Here we are in space or on another planet, or able to travel in time or read minds; we have encountered the aliens or made the fantastic discovery or invented the fantastic machine—now what?

What happens then may be a straight adventure story. On the other hand, it may be a story that develops the implications of the science fiction situation: what happens as a result of space or time travel, how telepathy or the marvelous machine works and how it affects society, the problems raised by the alien being or the alien planet. I will call this kind of story a *gimmick* story. Or a story may discuss the great philosophical questions that have plagued human beings since they first began to think: problems about religion, about human freedom, about human identity, and about surviving death. Problems of right and wrong for the individual and for society are often treated in science fiction, as well as problems about the scope and limits of human knowledge. A story that deals with such problems is what *I* call an *idea* story, but when people call science fiction "the literature of ideas" they usually mean to include what I call gimmick stories as well.

Is science fiction a literature of "ideas" in either the wide sense that includes gimmicks or in the narrow sense that includes only ideas of the kind that philosophers argue about? The only honest answer is that science fiction *can* be and often is about ideas in either the broad or the narrow sense, but it doesn't need to be. Without doing violence to the way we actually use words, you cannot deny the title science fiction to many stories not concerned with ideas in either of these senses —adventure stories, stories of character development, jokes and romps, and other "just-for-fun" stories without a trace of "idea" in either sense.

In fact, definitions of science fiction, such as "science fiction is a sub-genre of prose fiction which is distinguished from other kinds of fiction by the presence of an extrapolation of the human effects of an extrapolated science,"[1] or even "science fiction is the literature of ideas," are what logicians call *persuasive* definitions, attempts to say what the definer thinks science fiction ought to be rather than what it actually is. One could take any list of science fiction stories that have won prizes from science fiction fans or science fiction writers and find story after story that would not fit either definition. But I believe that any story on such lists would contain at least one of the several elements of science fiction we have been discussing and if it contained only one would contain it to a major degree. At any rate I am going to assume for the time being that the seven elements serve to give us a working definition of science fiction and go forward on that basis.

"Science fiction" is often abbreviated "SF"; if it makes you feel happier to call it "speculative fiction" or "science fantasy," go right ahead and do so. My definition of a science fiction story is just a story that contains at least one of the seven elements to an important degree, and you are free to argue that what I mean by science fiction is not what you mean by *real* science fiction. However, I think it is pretty close to what most readers, writers, and publishers of science fiction would recognize as science fiction.

We still have one major problem, distinguishing science fiction so defined from fantasy. Actually the fields are now and always have been so intertwined that a clear, sharp separation is almost impossible. It will help, however, to define some characteristic elements of fantasy. A story is fantasy if

it is set in the past before recorded history begins or at some time that cannot be put into a definite relationship with real time but resembles past eras of history; *or*

it involves magic (which can roughly be defined as the manipulation of nature by symbolic means); *or*

it contains persons or other creatures such that individuals like that one have been the subject of myths or legends; *or*

it involves marvelous events of which no scientific explanation is given or perhaps no scientific explanation seems possible.

Take, for example, *The Lord of the Rings*. Tolkien seems to intend it to be envisioned as taking place in the long ago past of our own world, but no exact relation of his legendary "history" to real history could be given. Tolkien's world of Middle-earth contains magic, wizards, such as Gandalf, and magical objects, such as the Ring. In Middle-earth there are Elves, Dwarves, and dragons, creatures from northern legend and myth. The marvelous events of the story are given no scientific explanation, and none seems possible for the story as told.

A story that contained only these elements, singly or in combination, would be recognized as a fantasy. If some of these elements are mixed with science fiction elements, you get mixed stories, which tend to be classified according to which elements are most prominent. For whatever reason, many of the best women writers of science fiction, Leigh Brackett, Catherine L. Moore, Andre Norton, Marion Zimmer Bradley, and Carolyn Cherryh, for instance, have tended to mix fantasy elements with science fiction elements in their writing. Usually a scientific explanation of the "magic" is offered, and although the cultures they write of are like those in our human past, they are often set in the future or on other planets, and this is usually enough to get their stories accepted as science fiction rather than fantasy.

Some symbols are extremely potent: the presence of a spaceship is almost enough by itself to make us feel that the story is science fiction;

the presence of a dragon almost enough to classify a story as fantasy. Anne McCaffrey gives a science fiction background to her dragonrider stories, but many readers seem to regard them as fantasy rather than science fiction, so powerful is the dragon as a symbol. However, most of the supposed irreconcilable differences between science fiction and fantasy (science fiction deals with the possible, fantasy with the impossible; science fiction is logical, fantasy is not) can be proved by many counterexamples not to exist.

To return to science fiction, there are many ways in which it can be subdivided. We have already mentioned adventure, gimmick, and idea stories; of course these are not mutually exclusive, and some of the best science fiction contains all three elements. Often we are most aware of the idea element in a story when we disagree with it: non-Christians object to the religious ideas in C. S. Lewis's "space trilogy" (and his Narnian fantasy stories). But unless we are extremely hidebound, which most readers of science fiction are not, we can enjoy reading about ideas even if we disagree with them.

Before we leave the question of to what extent science fiction is the literature of ideas, one final comment; it will not do as a definition of science fiction, for the reasons given, but it does express an important truth about science fiction: ideas *are* important in a lot of science fiction, and if you want to write a story involving ideas, science fiction or fantasy is probably your best choice. Lots of thinking about society and its problems has taken the form of science fiction: *utopian* stories, which picture an ideal society, or *dystopian* stories, which warn of how bad society could become. But science fiction has been used to express ideas about other important topics, religion, for example. One of the most influential Christian thinkers in the twentieth century was C. S. Lewis, and some of his most influential books are a science fiction trilogy and series of fantasy stories for children. Plenty of people have written antireligious science fiction or fiction expressing doubts and problems about religion, for example, the late James Blish. Science fiction is a natural vehicle for exploring ethics and for examining alternative lifestyles, or for whatever other ideas you want to explore.

Two things ought to be noted. First, science fiction, like philosophy, challenges our assumptions and preconceptions. If you plan to write a story challenging current thinking, you are far more likely to get it published if it is science fiction. A good deal of mainstream literature simply affirms values people already have—in fact, that is probably one of the social functions of literature. But in its constant search for new ideas, science fiction is ready to look at any challenge to or reversal of accepted ideas. The second thing to be aware of is that a story cannot *prove* or even *support* any idea. It cannot cite data, for in fiction the data can be invented to suit the author. If it gives detailed arguments or chains of reasoning, it ceases to be a story and becomes a disguised philosophical treatise. What a story *can* do is help us to *understand* an idea and help us see what it feels like to hold that idea.

There are other ways of categorizing science fiction that cut across the classification into adventure, gimmick, and idea stories. Take, for instance, stories of *exploration*. The exploration may be of strange planets, of different eras of human history, of other dimensions, and so on. The focus may be on the physical characteristics of the strange environment or the alien plants and animals or the alien persons that are encountered. An exploration story may be sheer adventure—one narrow escape after another from menaces contained in the alien environment. An exploration story can also be a gimmick story, in which the chief focus is on the curious and unique elements of the environment, which may pose intellectual as well as physical challenges. Or the exploration may be used to bring out ideas: the exploration itself may even be a kind of physical analogue of the search for truth or wisdom. C. S. Lewis, in the first two volumes of his "space trilogy," uses brilliantly imagined pictures of Mars and Venus essentially as backgrounds for dramas of ideas. But the physical background and the imagined inhabitants are vivid and exciting in their own right as well as being closely tied to the ideas of the story.

A kind of story that can overlap with the exploration story is the story of *social structure*. As suggested in some of the comments on the exploration story, one of the exotic elements is often the alien social structure. Where this is a major focus in an exploration story, the story fits into both categories, exploration and social structure. But many stories of social structure are set in the familiar environment of Earth and cannot be classified as stories of exploration without unduly stretching the meaning of "exploration."

The social structure can be used merely to create adventures for the protagonist: the society may have a "guild of assassins" or a dueling code merely to pose a threat to the life of the hero or heroine. Or ingenious social arrangements can be worked out merely for their intrinsic interest, making the story a gimmick story. But very often a story of social structure is a device to make an oblique comment on our own society. It is easy for a story of that kind to degenerate into a treatise or a tract, as indeed most classical stories of utopias and dystopias do at some point or other.

Another important kind of science fiction story is the *gadget* story, which centers around some marvelous machine or quasi-mechanical device. Isaac Asimov's robot stories can be classified mainly as gadget stories, and depending on the story, Asimov may be using the robots merely to tell a story of adventure or to explore the technical problems involved in "robotics" or to comment on social and ethical or even religious issues. And of course the gadget story may be combined with the exploration or social structure story.

Finally, some science fiction stories can only be described as *psychological* stories, or stories of character. Science fiction is often criticized for neglecting characterization, and the story of character change and development seems much more at home in contemporary, realistic fiction. But there have always been some science fiction stories that concentrate on psychology or character development. Stories of "supermen," such as Stapledon's *Odd John,* are often basically psychological studies of the alienated or unusual human individual. (Incidentally, I would classify "superman" stories as involving the "alien" theme, since supermen are by definition more than and other than human.)

Now how does all this relate to mythology? Plainly, if it is simply regarded as a kind of story, myth has a great deal in common with science fiction, and especially with fantasy. Myth, like fantasy, tends to be backward-looking, to set its stories in the remote past. Instead of space travel, it tends to have magical or mysterious means of travel, such as those employed by the gods in Homer or the mysterious gates to the Other World or Faerie or the Underworld found in some legends and fairy tales. Instead of a distant planet, a myth may be set in heaven or hell, Olympus or Hades, the land of Faerie or the Western Isles.

Time travel as such does not come into any myth, though there are "Rip van Winkle" stories in which a mortal wanders into an enchanted realm and returns to the world to find that many years have passed in what seemed a short time in the other world. In many myths and legends, gods or elves seem to have powers like those that would be called "psi" powers nowadays. Gods, elves, dragons, gryphons, and so on fit the classification of "alien" persons, whereas such things as magical rings and swords and helms and cloaks replace the machines of science fiction.

Myths served many functions in more primitive societies, and at least some of them were very similar to some of the purposes served today by science fiction and fantasy. Sheer entertainment is one such purpose. People have always enjoyed stories about fantastic and far-off things and people, whether in the form of travelers' tales, medieval and Renaissance romances, or today's science fiction and fantasy films, like *Star Wars* or *Dragonslayer*. One element in Homer's *Odyssey*, for example, is simply a story of adventure and exploration.

The element I have called the gimmick element is not especially strong in the higher mythology, where gods or magical objects seem to achieve their effects simply by being what they are. But in fairy tales there is often a sort of gimmick element in that the protagonist of the tale has a problem to solve in the face of what seems like overwhelming odds. How is the youngest son to win fame and fortune and the hand of the princess? How is the princess to recover her beloved who has been magicked away to some enchanted realm? Often the solution is a mixture of nature, wit, and magical help: for example, the princess takes a job as scullery maid in the enchanted palace where her beloved is held but then is befriended by an enchanted creature she has been kind to.

Obviously myths have been used to convey ideas of all kinds. Stories about the marital wranglings of Zeus and Hera or Aphrodite and Hephaestus could be used to make a comment on human husbands and wives. The protagonists of the stories about demigods and heroes often express cultural values. The heroes of Greek myth are often quick-witted as well as strong and brave. Odysseus is the paradigm of the thinker as hero, but even Hercules is more than a strongman. He cleanses the Augean stables by directing a river to do his work, for example, which needs ingenuity as well as strength.

Tolkien's mythology as expressed in *The Silmarillion* and in the background myths of *The Hobbit* and *The Lord of the Rings* probably owes most to his study of genuine original myth. Many writers on Tolkien have mentioned his debt to the myths and legends of northern Europe, but an influence equally strong or even stronger is Greek and Roman mythology. As we will see, Tolkien's Valar have a greater resemblance to the Olympian gods than to the Scandinavian gods such as Odin and Thor. For the details of his stories Tolkien has borrowed from many myths, but Greek and Roman language and literature kept a strong hold on his imagination. He writes in a letter that "I was brought up in the Classics and first discovered the sensation of literary pleasure in Homer."[2] Elsewhere he comments on the way in which the "marvelous aesthetic" of the Greek language ties together the Greek mythology into a unity[3]: this was a major objective of his own, making his invented languages give a unity to his mythic system. Later on, at the period when he wrote *The Lord of the Rings* and afterwards, Tolkien read at least some science fiction and modern fantasy. In 1967 he wrote:

I read quite a lot—or more truly, try to read many books (notably so-called Science Fiction and Fantasy). But I seldom find any modern books that hold my attention. There are exceptions. I have read all that E. R. Eddison wrote, in spite of his peculiarly bad nomenclature and personal philosophy. I was greatly taken by the book that was (I believe) the runner-up when *The L.R.* was given the Fantasy Award: *Death of Grass*. I enjoy the fiction of Isaac Azimov [*sic*]. Above these I was recently deeply engaged in the books of Marie Renault, especially the two about Theseus, *The King Must Die* and *The Bull from the Sea*. A few days ago I actually received a card of appreciation from her; perhaps the piece of "fan-mail" that gives me most pleasure.[4]

These comments, of course, were made after the writing of *The Lord of the Rings,* but they show the general *kind* of reading Tolkien enjoyed: Isaac Asimov's stories are typical science fiction (set in the future with space travel, off-Earth locations, etc.). Marie Renault's stories are based on Greek mythology, though they play down the magical and fantastic elements. Eddison's stories are set in a fantastic "alternative universe" and have a strong supernatural element.

One story we know Tolkien enjoyed before writing *The Lord of the Rings* was C. S. Lewis's Martian novel *Out of the Silent Planet*. Tolkien wrote a letter to a publisher in an effort to help Lewis get the book published.

I read the story in the original MS, and was so enthralled that I could do nothing else until I had finished it. . . . All the part about language and poetry —the glimpses of its Malacandrian nature and form—is very well done and extremely interesting, far superior to what one usually gets from travellers in untravelled regions. The language difficulty is usually slid over or fudged. Here it not only has verisimilitude, but underlying thought . . . I should have said that the story had for the more intelligent reader a great number of philosophical and mythical implications that enormously enhanced without detracting from the surface "adventure." I found the blend of *vera historia* with *mythos* irresistible. There are of course certain satirical elements, inevitable in any such traveller's tale and also a spice of satire on similar works of "scientific" fiction.[5]

This letter forms an interesting commentary on what Tolkien himself tried to accomplish and did accomplish in *The Lord of the Rings*: "philosophical and mythical implications that enormously enhanced without detracting from the surface 'adventure' . . . [a] blend of *vera historia* with *mythos*" are descriptions of Tolkien's best work as well as Lewis's.

In fact Tolkien's work and Lewis's are almost unique in the successful blending of these elements. There is plenty of science fiction that has philosophical elements, plenty of fantasy with mythical elements, but the blend of all three is rare. Ursula LeGuin in her Earthsea trilogy and Samuel R. Delany in his Neveryon books approach this blend most closely.

Tolkien is on record as disliking Lewis's Narnia books and also criticizing the concluding book of Lewis's "space trilogy," *That Hid-*

eous Strength, partly because of the influence Tolkien felt Charles Williams had on it.

The "space travel" trilogy . . . was basically foreign to Williams' kind of imagination. It was planned years before when we decided to divide: Lewis was to do space travel and I was to do time travel. . . . Publication dates are not a good guide. Williams' influence actually only appeared with his death: *That Hideous Strength,* the end of the trilogy which (good though it is in itself) I think spoiled it.[6]

There may have been a certain element of jealousy in Tolkien's attitude to Charles Williams. He wrote about Williams's relationship to Lewis in a letter to his son in 1963: "We were separated first by the sudden apparition of Charles Williams, then by his marriage."[7] Tolkien was tempermentally, I think, the sort of man who chooses a few close friends and sticks to them for life, whereas Lewis was inclined to expand his circle of friends. Tolkien says in a letter, "C. S. L. was my closest friend from about 1927 to 1940 and remains very dear to me —his death was a grievous blow. But in fact we saw less and less of one another after he came under the influence of Charles Williams and still less after his very strange marriage."[8] I am not sure that Lewis would ever have thought of Tolkien as "my closest friend": the note of exclusiveness is not like Lewis, but very like Tolkien.

As it happened it was the science fiction community that in an indirect and complicated way caused much of the wide public attention that came to *The Lord of the Rings.* The story was published in three books in hardcover by Unwin in England and Houghton Mifflin in the United States. It attracted some attention but seemed to have no wide public appeal. Donald A. Wollheim, a longtime science fiction fan, writer, and editor, was at this time (1965) editor in chief of Ace Books, a firm that published inexpensive paperbacks that were in many ways the successors of the pulp magazines (Ace had started as a magazine publisher). Wollheim admired *The Lord of the Rings* and thought that it would appeal to the readers of Ace science fiction, which included some fantasy and borderline science fiction–fantasy.

What happened next is still somewhat controversial. It is described from the point of view of Tolkien and his publishers in Humphrey Carpenter's biography of Tolkien:

. . . what Tolkien and others regarded as an American 'pirate' edition of *The Lord of the Rings* had been issued.

The publishers were Ace Books, who (when challenged) alleged there was nothing illegal in their paperback, even though it was printed entirely without the permission of Tolkien or his authorised publishers, and even though no royalty payment had been offered to the author.

Ace were already known as publishers of science fiction, and clearly a lot of people were going to buy their edition until an authorised paperback could be issued. An urgent request was sent to Tolkien to complete the revisions. . . .

In October 1965, the "authorised" paperback of *The Lord of the Rings* was published in America. . . . Each copy carried a message from Tolkien: "This paperback edition and no other has been published with my consent and cooperation. Those who approve of courtesy (at least) to living authors will purchase it and no other."

But this did not immediately produce the desired result. The Ballantine edition cost twenty cents per volume more than the Ace edition, and the American student buyers did not at first show a preference for it. Clearly something more would have to be done. . . . Tolkien himself played a prominent and efficient part in the campaign that now began . . . he began to include a note in all his replies to American readers informing them that the Ace edition was unauthorized and asking them to tell their friends. This soon had a remarkable effect. American readers not only began to refuse to buy the Ace edition but demanded . . . that booksellers remove it from their shelves.[9]

Another point of view is given in the lively and controversial "unauthorized" biography of Tolkien by Daniel Grotta:

One serious tactical mistake that Allen & Unwin made was in greatly underestimating the audience for *The Lord of the Rings*. The trilogy became an underground classic among science fiction and fantasy readers, many of whom could not afford $15 or more for a three-volume hardbound set. There had been a sizable paperback market for the work almost immediately after its initial publication in the mid-50s, but no paperback edition was forthcoming. This oversight by both Allen & Unwin and Houghton Mifflin created a vacuum that was filled by a less conservative publishing house, Ace Books. . . .

Ace Books was and still is a major paperback publisher of popular science fiction. . . . Wollheim knew about the underground popularity of *The Lord of the Rings* and wanted to get the rights to publish it in paperback. He quickly found out that the trilogy was not copyrighted in the United States and therefore, according to him, began lengthy and frustrating negotiations with Professor Tolkien through Allen & Unwin. Allen & Unwin was unenthusiastic, and Tolkien did not respond at all. When Wollheim finally advised his publisher, A.A. Wyn, of the situation, Wyn told him to go ahead and publish the trilogy. The Ace Books edition . . . went on sale in May, 1965. . . .

Ace's decision to publish the work in paperback was probably the best thing that ever happened to Tolkien. According to Donald Wollheim's wife, it "took off like a rocket," revealing the unrealized readership potential for an affordable edition of *The Lord of the Rings*. Despite the official acrimony and the charge of moral piracy, Tolkien profited handsomely from the entire affair. Technically, Ace Books was not obliged to give Tolkien a single penny for the rights to his books, but A.A. Wyn decided to set aside all the money that would have ordinarily gone to the author and establish a Tolkien Prize, which would encourage young writers of science fiction and fantasy. When Wollheim wrote to Tolkien of their intention to apply the $11,000 to a literary prize in his name, Tolkien responded and asked for the money himself. Since the agreement was between Ace and Tolkien, the entire $11,000 went directly to the professor. Ordinarily the author and original publisher share equally in any foreign rights; with three publishers—Allen & Unwin, Houghton Mifflin, and Ballantine Books—this meant that Tolkien received only 25 percent of the royalties from the official American edition. Since no other publishers were involved with Ace, Tolkien received 100 percent.[10]

The points not in dispute are that Tolkien's publishers had lost American copyright protection for *The Lord of the Rings* by importing too many "sheets" (unbound copies) of the book from England to be bound and published in the United States, and that Ace Books was within its legal rights in publishing a paperback edition without payment to Tolkien or his publishers. The question in dispute is whether they were morally justified in doing so.

Wollheim's side of the controversy, as stated in Grotta's book and confirmed in a letter to me, is that he and others had requested paper-back rights from Tolkien's publisher and been turned down. When it came to light that U.S. copyright protection for the work had been lost, it seemed to Wollheim that this explained the refusal: they could not sell rights they did not have. There seemed no reason to suppose that there would ever be an American paperback edition authorized by Houghton Mifflin. So Wollheim felt justified in going ahead with an Ace Books paperback edition. He was under no legal obligation to offer any royalties to Tolkien or Houghton Mifflin. The publisher could not have accepted any such royalties without in effect authorizing his edition, nor could Tolkien have accepted them without undercutting his publisher's position.

Tolkien and his publishers responded by waging a publicity cam-paign which emphasized the fact that Tolkien received no royalties from the Ace edition and by preparing a revised edition that could be protected under U.S. copyright law. The controversy over the Ace and Ballantine editions gave *The Lord of the Rings* a good deal of publicity and undoubtedly helped its growing sales. Ace Books eventually ceased publication of its edition. In a letter to W. H. Auden, Tolkien says:

May I intrude into this letter a note on Ace Books, since I have engaged to inform "my correspondents" of the situation. They in the event sent me a courteous letter and I signed an "amicable agreement" with them to accept their voluntary offer under no legal obligation: to pay a royalty at 4 per cent on all copies of their edition sold, and not to reprint it when exhausted (without my consent).[11]

In the end the whole affair has a somewhat comic aspect. Tolkien undoubtedly benefited. A paperback edition of *The Lord of the Rings* got printed in the United States that might have been published later or not at all if left to his American publishers. The controversy gave the book priceless publicity. And because the Ace payment was made directly to Tolkien, he got more of it than he would have otherwise. Standard contracts of that period gave the hardcover publisher 50 percent or so of payments for paperback publication, and 4 percent was a fairly standard royalty rate for most mass market paperbacks. Thus Tolkien got 4 percent instead of 2 percent of the money earned by the

Ace paperback and, I hope, got a somewhat better deal on the Ballantine paperback than he might otherwise have.

Humphrey Carpenter, Tolkien's biographer, concluded that the whole business had done more good than harm: "Ace had unwittingly done a service to Tolkien, for they had helped lift his book from the 'respectable' hard cover status in which it had languished for some years and had put it at the top of the popular bestsellers."[12]

To sum up our account of science fiction, fantasy, and myth in relation to Tolkien: all three have important elements in common, but each differs from the other in essential ways. Tolkien's work, though certainly not science fiction, is admired by many readers of science fiction. *The Lord of the Rings* not only is fantasy but is probably responsible for the current popularity of fantasy, which threatens to take over some of the market for science fiction. (Adult fantasy as a publishing category really started with the effort by Ballantine and other publishers to find "something like Tolkien" to satisfy the enormous market created by *The Lord of the Rings.*)

The effect of Tolkien's work on his readers has often been to restore the mythic dimension to their consciousness, even to the extent that some Tolkien enthusiasts dress in costumes and re-enact incidents from *The Lord of the Rings.* The old connection of myth and ritual has been partly restored. Tolkien may not have quite succeeded in making a mythology for *all* of England, but he has created a new mythology that lives in and for some of his readers.

4. Hobbits and Heroism

One function of myth is to convey moral values, and as we have seen, Tolkien himself gives as one purpose of his writing "the encouragement of good morals in this real world by the ancient device of exemplifying them in unfamiliar embodiments, that may tend to 'bring them home.' "[1] But how does Tolkien do this? To answer this question it is important to look at Tolkien's whole strategy in his major work, *The Lord of the Rings*. The first thing to realize is that the focus of the book, the "human interest," is not in the human characters, the Men, but in the Hobbits. The traditional kinds of heroes, Aragorn, for example, exist in the story partly to validate by their respect and approval the simple, dogged heroism of the Hobbits.

In many ways Tolkien "facets" character: each individual, and to some extent each race, represents one aspect of a complete human being. He has said specifically that the Elves represent certain human characteristics in isolation: "in fact exterior to my story Elves and Men are just different aspects of the Humane. . . . The Elves represent, as it were, the artistic, aesthetic and purely scientific aspects of human nature raised to a higher level than is actually seen in Men."[2]

Another kind of contrast is made between Men and Hobbits, with Men representing the traditional noble and knightly style of heroism and Hobbits the kind of courage exhibited by the ordinary person who rises to heroism in the face of challenge. Tolkien saw these two kinds of heroic style as interdependent and complementary.

This last great Tale, coming down from myth and legend to the earth is seen mainly through the eyes of Hobbits: it thus becomes in fact anthropocentric. But through Hobbits, not Men so-called because the last Tale is to exemplify most clearly a recurrent theme: the place in "world politics" of the unforeseen and unforeseeable acts of will and deeds of virtue of the apparently small, ungreat, forgotten in the places of the Wise and Great (good as well as evil). A moral of the whole . . . is the obvious one that without the high and noble the simple and vulgar is utterly mean; and without the simple and ordinary the noble and heroic is meaningless.[3]

To see how Tolkien develops this theme, consider his first book, *The Hobbit.* At the beginning Bilbo Baggins is a somewhat self-important little fellow, set in his ways and suspicious of anything outside his own limited sphere. He is bullied into going on an adventure with a band of Dwarves by Gandalf the wizard, but even in this first encounter he shows the beginnings of courage. After being terrified by talk of death and dragons, he has a fainting fit, but stung by the contempt shown by the Dwarves who have come to enlist his help on their quest, he offers to go along with them, even though he thinks that they have made a mistake in coming to him.

"I am quite sure you have come to the wrong house. As soon as I saw your funny faces on the door-step, I had my doubts. But treat it as the right one. Tell me what you want done, and I will try it, if I have to walk from here to the East of East and fight the wild were-worms in the Last Desert."[4]

In his next trial of courage, he is sent by the Dwarves to scout out a mysterious campfire that promises some hope of warmth on a miserable rainy night. He is easily captured by the Trolls who are sitting around the fire and has to be rescued by Gandalf, but at least he has had the courage to go when the Dwarves send him. His increased status is symbolized by a sword (only a dagger by human standards) that he receives as his share when the treasure of the Trolls is shared out.

Bilbo's next adventure begins when he and the Dwarves are captured by Goblins when they shelter for the night in a cave. It is Bilbo's yell that awakes Gandalf in the nick of time and enables the wizard to escape and later come to the rescue. But in the rescue Bilbo is separated from the others and wanders into the depths of the Goblin caverns, where he encounters a predatory creature, Gollum. Bilbo keeps him from attacking by the threat of his new-won sword. The ring of invisibility that Bilbo "accidentally" finds on his adventure is again a mark of his increased power, evidenced by his ability to trade riddles with Gollum and make the creature guide him out of the caverns.

When Bilbo does get free of the caverns, he looks for the Dwarves and does not at first find them. At the beginning of his adventure he might simply have abandoned his dangerous adventure and tried to get home. But already he has grown enough in moral stature so that

a very uncomfortable thought was growing within him. He wondered whether he ought not, now that he had the magic ring, to go back into the horrible, horrible, tunnels and look for his friends. He had just made up his mind that it was his duty, that he must turn back—and very miserable he felt about it—when he heard voices.[5]

The voices are those of the Dwarves, who have won free with Gandalf's help, and he does not have to carry out his decision. But the reader feels that he would have if he had not found the Dwarves. We are shown, however, that the Dwarves might not have done the same for him.

The dwarves were grumbling and Gandalf was saying that they could not possibly go on with their journey leaving Mr. Baggins in the hands of the goblins, without trying to find out if he was alive or dead and without trying to rescue him. . . . The dwarves wanted to know why he had ever been brought at all. . . . "He has been more trouble than use so far," said one. "If we have to go back now into those abominable tunnels to look for him, then drat him, I say."[6]

We are not told Bilbo's reaction to this, but the Dwarves are impressed by his escape and the fact that he appears to have crept quietly up on them without their lookout spotting him (he does not tell them about the magic ring). They begin to depend on him, and even though they are rescued from their next scrape by eagles summoned by Gandalf, the Dwarves rely on Bilbo, especially after Gandalf leaves them at the entrance to the great and grim forest of Mirkwood.

In Mirkwood the Dwarves leave the safe path, against Gandalf's advice, and are captured by giant spiders. With his sword, Bilbo manages to kill the spider who attacks him, and

somehow the killing of the giant spider, all alone by himself in the dark without the help of the wizard or the dwarves or of anyone else, made a great difference to Mr. Baggins. He felt a different person, and much fiercer and bolder in spite of an empty stomach. . . . The forest was grim and silent, but obviously he had first of all to look for his friends.[7]

Tolkien makes Bilbo's increasing courage plausible to us in two ways —first, by showing us its cause and, second, by reminding us of Bilbo's limitations—his empty stomach and a little later his loneliness without his companions. The idealized heroes of some fantasies never seem to worry about such ordinary things as hunger and loneliness. But because of Bilbo's very ordinariness, we are often reminded of the uncomfortable and even comic side of adventure—and at the same time reminded that ordinary people can act heroically.

Bilbo does rescue the Dwarves with the use of his sword and his magic ring, as well as his wits and a skill at throwing stones he learned as a young Hobbit. The rescue is not a matter of a single hero attacking a group of monsters and hewing them limb from limb: it involves the use of the magic ring to confuse the spiders and lead them away from their prey; Bilbo then creeps back and frees the Dwarves.

The Dwarves are next captured by the Elves who live in the woods, basically good creatures but hostile to Dwarves and protective of their domain. Bilbo frees them by the use of his ring and his wits, and they arrive at the threshold of their goal—the town nearest to the mountain where the dragon broods on his heap of treasure. It is this treasure, stolen from the Dwarves, that they have journeyed to recover. The Dwarves are welcomed by the town and, with ponies supplied by the townspeople, journey to the mountain itself and find the side entrance to the dwarf-caverns inside the mountain where the dragon guards the treasure.

They have not come to fight the dragon but to steal back some of their own treasure. Bilbo is sent down into the dragon's stronghold to begin taking some treasure.

Then the hobbit slipped on his ring and, warned by the echoes to take more than a hobbit's care to make no sound, he crept noiselessly down, down into the dark. He was trembling with fear, but his little face was set and grim. Already he was a very different hobbit from the one that had run out without a pocket-handkerchief from Bag End long ago. He had not had a pocket-handkerchief for ages. He loosened his dagger in its sheath, tightened his belt and went on. . . . Going on from there was the bravest thing he ever did. The tremendous things that happened afterwards were as nothing compared to it. He fought the real battle in the tunnel alone, before he even saw the vast danger that lay in wait.[8]

Bilbo does manage to steal a cup from the treasure, which enrages the dragon, who flies out of his cave and nearly catches the Dwarves waiting outside. They scurry into the tunnel, realizing that they have little chance of escaping with any treasure while Smaug, the dragon, lives. Bilbo volunteers to go on another scouting mission.

"Getting rid of dragons is not at all in my line [Bilbo says], but I will do my best to think about it. Personally I have no hopes at all, and wish I was safe back home. . . . I have got my ring and will creep down . . . and see what he is up to. Perhaps something will turn up." . . . Naturally the dwarves accepted the offer eagerly. Already they had come to respect little Bilbo. Now he had become the real leader in their adventure.[9]

This reconnaissance is a partial disaster, because it sends Smaug off to attack the townspeople who had befriended the Dwarves. However, Bilbo has seen a weak spot in the dragon's armor, and word of it gets back to one of the town's defenders, who kills the dragon with an arrow when the monster attacks the town. Thus Bilbo is the indirect cause of the dragon's removal, though he never gets any thanks for it. But now the struggle moves from the traditional heroic to the political. With the dragon dead, five armies converge on the dragon's lair to claim the treasure: the Men from the town, Elves from the wood, Dwarves from the North, and the Goblins and their wolflike allies.

Men and Elves arrive first, but the Dwarves with Bilbo refuse to share the treasure, hoping for help from their Dwarvish allies to the North. Now Bilbo shows a moral courage to match the physical courage he has shown earlier. To end the impasse, he takes possession of one piece of the treasure particularly beloved by the leader of the Dwarves and delivers it to the Elves and Men who are besieging the Dwarves, to use as a bargaining point. Then he goes back to the Dwarves to face the consequences of his action. Thorin, leader of the Dwarves, is enraged by what he sees as treachery, and Bilbo escapes execution by the Dwarves only with the aid of Gandalf.

The kind of courage exhibited by Bilbo in this incident is not the usual heroism of the folktales. He has to make a lonely moral decision as to rights and wrongs in a complex situation, devise a plan with no help or support from those who should be his friends, and carry it out alone. His return to face the rage of the Dwarves shows another kind of courage, exhibiting a sense of honor and obligation that is chivalrous, almost quixotic. But Bilbo does not speak of honor, he speaks of what he owes to his friends, the "friends" who have done so much less for him than he for them. For all his pretense sometimes to be "business-like" and "sensible," friendship is not a business matter for Bilbo: for him friendship involves giving even if you do not receive. The true word for what he calls friendship is love, the sort of love spoken of by Paul in his First Letter to the Corinthians that "endures long and is kind . . . it is not self-seeking . . . nor does it take account of a wrong that is suffered. It takes no pleasure in injustice, but sides happily with truth."10

The coming of the Goblins and their allies returns us from the political to the heroic; the armies of Dwarves, Elves, and Men fight together against the forces of evil and win, with the help of the eagles. At the end Dwarves, Elves, and Men are victorious, and their differences are reconciled. Bilbo is also reconciled with Thorin and the other Dwarves. Thorin's dying words pay tribute to Bilbo's courage but also to his humane qualities.

"There is more in you than you know, child of the kindly West. Some courage and some wisdom, blended in measure. If more of us valued food and cheer and song above hoarded gold, it would be a merrier world. But sad or merry, I must leave it now. Farewell."11

Through all this Bilbo retains his humility and good sense, scarcely needing Gandalf's reminder at the end of the story.

"You are a very fine person, Mr. Baggins, and I am very fond of you: but you are only quite a little fellow in a wide world after all."
"Thank goodness," said Bilbo, laughing, and handed him the tobacco-jar.12

We will see all of Bilbo's virtues again in the Hobbits in *The Lord of the Rings,* but it is worthwhile to pause here and sum up what we have learned from Tolkien's first story. Bilbo is not a "natural" hero: his life up to the beginning of the story has not demanded heroism. He needs to be bullied into adventure by Gandalf and at first does little more than allow himself to be pushed into dangerous situations by the Dwarves, who have a tendency to let Bilbo, the outsider, do the dirty work. (The Dwarves are not only united as Dwarves but are all members of one extended family.) However, Bilbo does do his best when in these dangerous situations, and with each small and partial success his confidence grows.

To a certain extent Gandalf functions as a parental figure, pushing Bilbo to get him started but then stepping back to let Bilbo struggle and learn on his own. After Bilbo's discovery of the ring and his success in escaping from Gollum and the Goblins on his own, Gandalf soon removes himself entirely and lets Bilbo gradually take his place as leader and protector of the Dwarves.

In taking on this responsibility, Bilbo gradually grows fond of his grumbling, ungrateful companions and exhibits loyalty to them in situations in which they do little to deserve his loyalty. Gradually Bilbo assumes the parental role in place of Gandalf until, as we have seen, "he had become the real leader in their adventures."

The Dwarves never entirely acknowledge this fact explicitly, however, and when lust for the treasure overcomes them, they soon rebel against Bilbo's attempts to make a sensible peace. So Bilbo has little chance to develop a swelled head or become autocratic. However, he does receive praise from the Elf king, from Gandalf, and eventually from the Dwarves, and keeps his modest and sensible attitude despite it. So the characteristic virtues of Bilbo might be summed up as courage, loyalty, and humility—courage toward dangers and enemies, loyalty and love to friends, humility with regard to his own qualities and achievements.

These characteristics also apply to the Hobbits we encounter in *The Lord of the Rings,* but they are found to a greater extent in Sam than in any of the other characters. This may seem surprising, for at the beginning Sam seems only a minor, comic character, and Frodo seems to be the "hero" of the tale. Nor is this impression entirely mistaken: Frodo is the Ring-bearer and in one sense the most important character in the story. But in another way Sam is the central character, as some of Tolkien's comments in letters tell us. When *The Lord of the Rings* was still being written, he wrote to his son Christopher:

Sam is the most closely drawn character, the successor to Bilbo of the first book, the genuine hobbit. Frodo is not so interesting, because he has to be highminded, and has, as it were, a vocation. The book will probably end up with Sam. Frodo will naturally become too ennobled and rarified by the achievement of the great Quest and will pass West with all the great figures but Sam will settle down to the Shire and gardens and inns.[13]

In the event, this is just how *The Lord of the Rings* ends—with Frodo passing to the West and Sam returning home to the Shire. At one point in a later letter, Tolkien refers to Sam as the "chief character" of the story.[14]

However, at first the focus is certainly on Frodo. The magic ring that Bilbo has found in *The Hobbit* has turned out to be *the* Ring, the Ring of Power into which Sauron, the Dark Lord, has put a good deal of his own power, the ring that rules the other magical rings held by Men and Elves. Bilbo is persuaded by Gandalf to leave this ring to Frodo, his nephew, when Bilbo leaves the Shire, the land of the Hobbits. We find Bilbo later in the story living at Rivendell, one of the last outposts of the Elves in Middle-earth. Frodo is warned by Gandalf that he is accepting a dangerous gift, but he accepts it to relieve Bilbo of a burden and because he trusts the wisdom of Gandalf.

At first we see Gandalf as again a parent figure and Frodo as a child figure. At first he merely reacts to events, leaving Bilbo's home, now his, for a remote part of the Shire and then fleeing to Rivendell as emissaries of the Dark Lord pursue him, trying to capture the Ring. The weaknesses he shows at this stage are childish ones—putting off his departure despite Gandalf's warnings, giving away information by "showing off" at Bree. After this incident, he finds another parent figure, Aragorn, the descendant of the ancient kings of the land, who helps him on the next stage of his journey.

However, by the time he gets to Bree, he has had to do some growing up already. Instead of slipping away quietly and alone, he finds himself with three companions, his servant Sam and his friends Merry and Pippin. The little band is a help but also a responsibility. They are loyal to him but not subservient to him.

"It all depends on what you want [Merry says]. . . . You can trust us to stick to you through thick and thin—to the bitter end. And you can trust us to keep any secret of yours—closer than you keep it yourself. But you cannot trust us to let you face trouble alone, and go off without a word. We are your friends, Frodo. Anyway; there it is. We know most of what Gandalf has told you. We know a great deal about the Ring. We are horribly afraid—but we are coming with you—or following you like hounds.[15]

So Frodo, like Bilbo earlier, finds himself thrust into a position of responsibility for others. His leadership is soon put to the test, for in the Wild Lands between the Shire and Bree, Frodo and his companions are captured by undead creatures who live in great burial mounds from the past, the Barrow-wights. Frodo awakes to find himself laid out like the corpse of a king, with his companions near him sleeping or entranced. Frodo is tempted to abandon his companions and win free with the aid of the Ring.

A wild thought of escape came to him. He wondered if he put on the Ring whether the Barrow-wight would miss him, and he might find some way out. He thought of himself running free over the grass, grieving for Merry, and Sam, and Pippin, but free and alive himself. Gandalf would admit that there had been nothing else he could do.[16]

Frodo resists the temptation and escapes with his companions, but the temptation is by no means simple. Which is more important—his mission to keep the Ring out of the power of the Dark Lord or his loyalty to his friends? At a later point he is to face this decision in another form.

After he has resisted the temptation to flee and fought off one attack by a Barrow-wight, Frodo calls on and is rescued by Tom Bombadil, a comical but powerful being who has rescued the Hobbits from an earlier danger. The two incidents together are rather like Bilbo's early adventure with the Trolls: Frodo is rescued by a powerful outside force rather than by his own efforts. The childlike aspect of Frodo and the other Hobbits is emphasized at this point in the story when Tom Bombadil after his rescue tells them to take off the ancient garments the Barrow-wights have clothed them in and run naked in the grass. This is partly to dispel the enchantments that hold them by the power of the natural forces (such as sun and wind) that Tom is akin to and to some extent personifies. But it is also like the way one might treat a child after a terrifying experience:

"Run and play in the sun, forget what happened."

When they arrive at Bree, where Men and Hobbits live together in friendship, Pippin lets down his guard and begins to talk too much in the common room at the inn. In an effort to silence him, Frodo stands up and makes a speech thanking the company for their welcome. Then, at a loss what to do next, he responds to requests to sing a song. Singing and drinking put Frodo off his guard, and he "accidentally" puts the Ring on his finger and disappears, betraying more than Pippin would have by his words.

The Hobbits are now helped by Aragorn, descendant of the ancient kings and member of a band of Men who protect the peaceful lands by fighting the evil things in the Wild Lands on their borders. The Hobbits win through to Rivendell despite several attacks by the forces of evil: Frodo shows courage but largely lets himself be guided and guarded by Aragorn.

Safe in Rivendell, Frodo must make a vital decision: whether to hand over the Ring to others, or continue to be the Ring-bearer, at peril of death or enslavement to the Dark Lord. For the decision of the wisest enemies of evil is that the only course is to take the Ring into the Dark Lord's stronghold of Mordor and destroy it in the fires in which it was made. The Ring cannot be safely used against the Dark Lord, for it contains not just power but the evil power of the Dark Lord. Even if this power could be turned against its owner, the one who wielded the Ring to defeat him would eventually become evil.

The idea that those who use evil means to destroy evil become like the enemy they are fighting is central to Tolkien's thinking and writing. During World War II he wrote to his son about some ways in which the defenders of freedom seemed to be aping their Nazi adversaries and drew a moral from his own work, "You can't fight the Enemy with his own Ring without turning into an Enemy, but unfortunately Gandalf's wisdom seems long ago to have passed with him into the True West."[17]

At several points in the story, good and powerful characters, Gandalf among them, refuse to take the Ring, aware that they might be tempted to use it and fall into its trap. One of Frodo's qualification's for the task of Ring-bearer is his knowledge of his own limitations: up to the very end, he is aware that he is not great or powerful enough to take the Ring and wield it against its maker. As with Bilbo, part of Frodo's strength is humility.

Frodo does volunteer to carry the Ring to Mordor to destroy it, and his offer is accepted. He sets off with eight companions, and though he faces many dangers, he has both Aragorn and Gandalf with him and can be a follower rather than a leader. But in the Mines of Moria Gandalf is lost to them, seemingly killed in defending the others from a powerful evil being. The remainder of the Fellowship find rest and refuge and almost forget their grief for Gandalf in the beauty and wonder of Lothlórien, the greatest remaining stronghold of the Elves on Middle-earth.

But when they leave Lothlórien, disagreements begin about which route to take, and Boromir, a prince of the Men of Gondor, falls prey to the temptation of the Ring and tries to take it from Frodo. Frodo also feels the force of the Dark Lord's mind probing, searching for the Ring. Frodo escapes Boromir, fights off the impulse to submit to the Dark Lord, and sets off alone to carry out his mission. At the last moment Sam joins him, but Frodo is the leader—on his own at last.

His motive for going on alone is not pride, or even the feeling that one or two might escape notice where a larger group would not. Rather, he feels that the corrupting power of the Ring is responsible for the disagreements among the Fellowship and for Boromir's attempt to seize the Ring.

A great weariness was on him, but his will was firm and his heart lighter. He spoke aloud to himself, "I will do now what I must," he said. "This at least is plain: the evil of the Ring is already at work even in the Company and the Ring must leave them before it does more harm. I will go alone. Some I cannot trust, and those I can trust are too dear to me."[18]

In other words, his motive for going on alone is the same as his motive for taking the Ring in the first place: to help those he loves and because he feels that the responsibility has fallen on him. It is interesting that he mentions as those "too dear to me" the three other Hobbits and Aragorn, who has helped and defended him in the past. Boromir has "fallen into evil," as he says, and the Elf Legolas and the

Dwarf Gimli do not come to his mind as among those too dear to him to risk. Frodo loves the Elves and likes the Dwarves, but his greatest love is for his own folk, the Hobbits, and for a few like Gandalf and Aragorn who have been quasi-parental figures to him. This is just to say that Frodo is a limited being, not God. Christ in traditional Christian theology dies for all human beings individually; Frodo is willing to lay down his life for all those threatened by evil, but especially for his own folk and his own friends.

Yet in many ways Frodo's journey to Mordor is an echo, conscious or unconscious on Tolkien's part, of Christ's journey to Golgotha. One preparation for the Way of the Cross imagery in the last part of the story is the re-introduction of Gollum, whom Bilbo met long ago in the caverns of the Goblins. We have learned earlier that Gollum was originally a Hobbit named Sméagol, who accidentally found the Ring long years ago, killed a friend to get possession of it, and has been possessed and obsessed by it ever since. Now he is tracking Frodo in hopes of recovering the Ring, which he calls his "Precious." But Gollum is also being used as a tool by the Dark Lord, a hunting animal that may be allowed to snatch the Ring from Frodo but will not be allowed to keep it.

When Frodo finally meets Gollum face to face, he uses the power of the Ring to establish an ascendancy over him but also treats him with kindness, so that Gollum is torn between a growing love for Frodo and his ravenous desire for the Ring. Sam is both mistrustful of Gollum and jealous of him: one of Tolkien's very perceptive moral insights in the book is in his account of the way in which Sam's own devotion to Frodo is the innocent means of aborting Gollum's possible reformation. Tolkien speaks of "the tragedy of Gollum who . . . came within a hair of repentance—but for one rough word from Sam"[19] and elsewhere of "Gollum's failure (just) to repent when interrupted by Sam: this seems to me really like the *real* world in which the instruments of just retribution are seldom themselves just and holy and the good are often stumbling blocks."[20]

Partly, the attachment of Gollum to Sam and Frodo as their guide and helper is a preparation for the final betrayal by Gollum: to taste the depths of suffering, Frodo must be betrayed by one in whom he put his trust, as Christ was betrayed by Judas. Gollum also serves as a warning: if Frodo or Bilbo allowed themselves to yield to the power of the Ring, they would become like Gollum, enslaved by it rather than becoming its Master.

Indeed, Tolkien may intend to suggest that in a sense the Dark Lord himself is the slave rather than the master of his own evil power. For evil is in the end a rejection of *every* good, including freedom: the lustful man or woman becomes a slave of lust; the vengeful become slaves of their hatred; and so on. The romantic picture of evil that some have seen in Milton's *Paradise Lost* is an illusion. Evil says, "Better to reign in hell than serve in heaven," but in hell, no one but the Prince of Evil ever seems to reign, and that reign is an illusion too. Every one of the servants of Sauron, the Dark Lord, is a slave, and in the end Sauron himself is a slave to his own fear and hate.

As Frodo comes closer to Mordor, he is led into a trap by Gollum and rendered unconscious by the bite of a giant spider, then captured by the ones who guard Mordor. His physical sufferings parallel those of Christ: he is imprisoned, stripped of his garments, mocked, and whipped. Even after Sam rescues him and they resume their journey to the fires of the Crack of Doom to destroy the Ring, Frodo's sufferings continue. He is terribly weary, and the Ring becomes a more and more intolerable burden. Frodo's journey now powerfully recalls Christ's carrying of the cross.

Whether this is intentional on Tolkien's part is hard to say. As a Catholic of a rather traditional kind, Tolkien would have been familiar with the Rosary, a form of prayer in which beads and spoken prayers occupy the body and the surface of the mind while the person praying meditates on various "mysteries"—incidents from the life of Christ and his mother, Mary. The five "sorrowful mysteries" are Christ's agony of mind in the Garden of Gethsemane, his whipping by the Roman soldiers and their crowning of him with thorns, the carrying of the cross, and Christ's crucifixion and death. These are natural images of sacrificial suffering for any Catholic, but they also represent all the basic kinds of suffering: mental anguish, physical pain, being mocked, wearily carrying a burden, death in agony. Almost any great suffering will involve most of these in some way: all of them could be distinguished, for example, in the suffering of the Jews in Nazi concentration camps. So it is not clear if Tolkien consciously intended the reminder of Christ's suffering or merely tried to convey archetypal agony.

Frodo, of course, does not die. More surprisingly, he does not persevere to the end: at the last moment his will fails, and he is saved only by a seeming accident from undoing all the good of his mission. This is so important a point that we will have to discuss it at length in the next chapter. But to sum up the discussion of "Hobbits and heroism": both Bilbo and Frodo are examples of ordinary persons rising to heroism when it is demanded of them. The original motive of their heroism is loyalty and love of friends. Their realization of their own limitations, their common sense and humility, keeps them from the rashness that is the excess of the virtue of courage, the megalomania that is the downfall of some more conventionally heroic figures such as Boromir. Their courage is moral as well as physical: Bilbo is willing to bear the reproaches of his friends to try for a just peace. Frodo rejects the seemingly good advice of Sam and others and forgives and trusts Gollum. And in the last analysis, their self-sacrificing love rises to such heights as to be comparable to the greatest love the world has known.

5. Beyond Heroism

Frodo in one sense fails. That surprising fact is in itself an answer to those who think *The Lord of the Rings* is morally simplistic. When he finally reaches the object of his journey, the great fires within Mount Doom that alone can destroy the Ring:

Frodo . . . spoke with a clear voice, a voice clearer and more powerful than Sam had ever heard him use, and it rose above the throb and turmoil of Mount Doom, ringing in the roof and walls.

"I have come," he said. "But I do not choose now to do what I came to do. I will not do this deed. The Ring is mine!" And suddenly as he set it on his finger, he vanished. . . . And far away, as Frodo put on the Ring and claimed it as his own . . . the Tower trembled from its foundations to its proud and bitter crown. The Dark Lord was suddenly aware of him. Then his wrath blazed in consuming flame, but his fear rose like a vast black smoke to choke him. For he knew his deadly peril and the thread upon which his doom now hung.[1]

Could Frodo actually have taken the power and become a new Dark Lord, which is the temptation that the Ring holds out? In a letter Tolkein says:

When Sauron was aware of the seizure of the Ring his one hope was in its power: that the claimant would be unable to relinquish it until Sauron had time to deal with him. Frodo . . . would then probably . . . cast himself with the Ring in the abyss. If not he would of course have completely failed. . . . Sauron sent the Ring-wraiths . . . [their] errand was to remove Frodo from the crack. Once he lost the power or opportunity to *destroy* the Ring the end could not be in doubt . . . Frodo had become a considerable person, but of a special kind: in spiritual enlargement rather than in increase in physical or mental power . . . He needed time, much time before he could control the Ring . . . before his will and arrogance could grow to a status where it could dominate other major hostile wills. Even so for a long time his acts and commands would still have to seem "good" to him, to be for the benefit of others besides himself.[2]

This, by the way, is an interesting insight into why the power of the Ring is evil: its power is the power to dominate other wills, to enslave others. Even if the power were supposedly exercised for the good of others, its use would be evil: one cannot make others good by dominating their wills. Frodo has very nearly been victorious over the evil in Gollum by his kindness and trust. Gollum chose not to be saved, but merely dominating his will by power would have given him no chance to make a decision for good or evil.

Frodo has failed with Gollum, but his failure is fruitful; for at this moment Gollum leaps on Frodo, bites off the finger on which Frodo wears the Ring, and falls into the fires, destroying himself and the Ring. Frodo, though maimed, is saved both physically and mentally: Sam saves him from the fire, and with the Ring gone his mind clears and he realizes the folly of trying to claim the Ring.

There was Frodo, pale and worn, and yet himself again: and in his eyes there was peace now, neither strain of will, nor madness, nor any fear. His burden was taken away . . . he was himself again, he was free.[3]

To some this may seem a contrived solution, a deus ex machina solution. But Tolkien argued in letters to various critics that the solution was carefully prepared for and integrated into the story, and that Frodo deserved the admiration that Aragorn and others give him.

Frodo indeed "failed" as a hero, as conceived by simple minds: he did not endure to the end: he gave in, ratted. I do not say "simple minds" with contempt: they often see with clarity the simple truth and the absolute ideal to which effort must be directed, even if it is unattainable. Their weakness, however, is twofold. They do not perceive the complexity of any given situation in Time, in which an absolute ideal is enmeshed. They tend to forget . . . Pity or Mercy, which is an absolute requirement in moral judgement . . . we must estimate the limits of another's strength and weigh this against the force of particular circumstances. I do not think that Frodo's was a *moral* failure. At the last moment the pressure of the Ring would reach a maximum —impossible . . . for anyone to resist. . . . Frodo had done what he could and spent himself completely.[4]

Furthermore, Tolkien points out that Gollum's action was the outcome of earlier actions by Frodo.

At this point the "salvation" of the world and Frodo's own "salvation" is achieved by his previous *pity* and forgiveness of injury. At any point any prudent person would have told Frodo that Gollum would certainly betray him, and could rob him in the end. To "pity" him, to forbear to kill him, was a piece of folly or a mystical belief in the ultimate value-in-itself of pity and generosity even if disastrous in the world of time. He did rob him and injure him in the end—but by a "grace," that last betrayal was at a precise juncture when the final evil deed was the most beneficial thing anyone could have done for Frodo! By a situation created by his "forgiveness" he was saved himself and relieved of his burden. He was very justly accorded the highest honors.[5]

I submit that, in contrast to the psychological depth of this, not only most other tales of heroism but a good deal of what is called literature seems simplistic. Creation of the flawed heroes or antiheroes of much modern writing involves no great moral insight: it is no news that we often fall short of the ideal. But Tolkien's picture of a hero who fails, but succeeds after all because of his willingness to take a chance on another person, is both subtle and profoundly true to life. The heroes of some traditional tales are simplistic, but so are the antiheroes of many modern tales: romantic pessimism is as false to life as romantic optimism.

There are, in contrast to Frodo, a number of characters in *The Lord of the Rings* who must be regarded as moral failures, among them a Man, Denethor, a wizard, Saruman, and Gollum, the Hobbit who has become a monster. Furthermore, there are several pictures of persons who take a wrong turn but finally repent, including Boromir and Théoden. It will be worthwhile to briefly examine each of these characters and the double or triple contrasts that Tolkien makes with them and other characters.

Denethor, for example, is the ruler of Gondor, even though in theory his line of rulers are only stewards, ruling in the absence of the ancient kings whose descendant Aragorn is. Denethor, who rejects Gandalf's wisdom, falls victim to the enemy and eventually dies unrepentant. He is contrasted with Théoden, King of Rohan, who accepts Gandalf's help, rouses himself to new life, and dies heroically in battle. Denethor is also contrasted with his own sons, Boromir, who

shares his faults but repents, and Faramir, who represents what Denethor should have been. Furthermore, Tolkien uses the device of having Merry become a squire in Théoden's service and Pippin a squire
in Denethor's service, so that the Hobbits' courage and humility can
serve as a contrast to Denethor's pride and a counterpoint to
Théoden's reawakening.

Both Denethor and Théoden demonstrate hostility and arrogance on
their first meeting with Gandalf. But Théoden's suspicion of Gandalf
is due to overreliance on an evil counselor, Gríma Wormtongue, a tool
of Sauron. Gandalf is able to appeal to Théoden's better nature, get him
to see Gríma for what he is, and cast off the despair and inertia that
Gríma's plotting has imposed on him. Denethor's pride is more deep-
rooted and is partly due to the fact that in trying to learn more about
Sauron he has become fascinated with the power of evil and has
gradually fallen under its spell.

On their meeting with Denethor on their arrival in Gondor, Gandalf
warns Pippin:

"Be careful of your words, Master Peregrin! This is no time for hobbit
pertness. Théoden is a kindly old man. Denethor is of another sort, proud and
subtle, a man of far greater lineage and power, though he is not called a king.
But he will speak most to you and question you much, since you can tell him
of his son Boromir. He loved him greatly: too much perhaps and the more
so because they were unlike."[6]

Boromir, though like his father in pride and masterfulness, was able
to admit his error in trying to seize the Ring from Frodo. He gave his
life trying to defend the two remaining Hobbits from the Orcs, and
in gratitude for this, Pippin offers his allegiance to Denethor. Perhaps
Denethor is somewhat moved by this, but he accepts Pippin's impulsive
offer partly to get information from him, as a move in his game of
mastery.

"You are now sworn to his service [Gandalf says to Pippin]. I do not know
what put it into your head, or your heart, to do that. But it was well done.
I did not hinder it, for generous deed should not be checked by cold counsel.
It touched his heart . . . [but] there is another side to it. You are at his command
and he will not forget."[7]

Denethor has great powers and is inclined to trust to them and to his own sense of what is important.

"Pride would be folly that disdained help and counsel at need [he tells Gandalf], but you deal out such gifts according to your own designs. Yet the Lord of Gondor is not to be made the tool of other men's purposes, however worthy. And for him there is no purpose higher in the world as it now stands than the good of Gondor: and the rule of Gondor, my Lord, is mine."[8]

Denethor is in a way identifying himself with Gondor; he "serves" Gondor but thinks of it as his. He is very close to saying, and thinking, "There is no purpose higher in the world than my rule." And that is a sentiment that the Dark Lord could express too—except that each means *his* rule to prevail.

Gandalf, in contrast, takes his responsibilities differently: he was willing to lay down his life for his companions in the Mines of Moria.

"The rule of no realm is mine, neither of Gondor or any other, great or small [he replies to Denethor]. But all worthy things that are in peril as the world now stands, those are my care. And for my part, I shall not wholly fail in my task, though Gondor should perish, if anything passes through this night that can still grow fair or bear fruit in the days to come. For I also am a steward. Did you not know?"[9]

Pippin's generous gesture and Gandalf's selfless stewardship contrast in different ways with Denethor's pride. If he could only, as Pippin does, make a generous gesture without thought of consequences or, as Gandalf does, serve the good of others selflessly, he could be a great force on the side of good. But he trusts to himself and his own power and cunning, and when these fail, he despairs and kills himself. Just before he dies, he says:

"I would have things as they were all the days of my life . . . and in the days of my long-fathers before me: to be the Lord of this city and leave my choice to a son after me. . . . But if doom denies this to me, then I will have *naught:* neither life diminished nor love halved nor honor abated."[10]

This is the true voice of pride: either things as *I* want them or nothing. It is the voice of the spoiled child, the adult egomaniac, the sinner who will not repent.

Another character who is pictured as rejecting a chance to turn away from destruction is Saruman the wizard. Like Denethor he is great and powerful; like Denethor he trusts to his own strength to contend with Sauron; and like Denethor his attempts to learn more about his enemy have laid him open to the Dark Lord's influence. We see him first trying to corrupt Gandalf, persuade him to join in Saruman's own betrayal of the forces of good to the Dark Lord.

"There is one choice before you, before us. We may join with that Power. It would be wise, Gandalf. There is hope that way. Its victory is at hand: and there will be rich reward for those that aided it. As the Power grows its proved friends will grow: and the Wise, such as you and I, may with patience come to control it. We can bide our time, we can keep our thoughts in our hearts, deploring maybe evils done by the way, but approving the high and ultimate purpose: Knowledge, Rule, Order. . . . There need not be, there would not be any real change in our designs, only in our means."[11]

At this stage Saruman may believe his own propaganda, but notice already that "Knowledge, Rule, and Order" mean *Saruman's* knowledge, rule, and order, just as Denethor's "highest purpose" is his own rule. We next see Saruman after his tower has been besieged and conquered by Gandalf and his allies. Gandalf gives him a chance to repent, but Saruman refuses. As Gandalf says:

"I gave him a last choice and a fair one: to renounce both Mordor and his private schemes and make amends by helping us in our need. He knows our need, none better. Great service he could have rendered. But he has chosen to withhold it. . . . He will not serve, only command."[12]

Again, the distinctive note of pride is sounded, "He will not serve, only command." Yet just as Denethor's pride only leads him to destruction, Saruman's attempt to use the Dark Lord's power for his own purposes leads to his destruction. We see him last as a wandering beggar who tries to get his revenge on Gandalf and the Hobbits by corrupting the Shire, the homeland of the Hobbits.

"You make me laugh, you hobbit lordlings. . . . You thought you had done very well out of it all and could just amble back and have a quiet time in the country. Saruman's home could be wrecked and he could be turned out, but no one could touch yours. . . . Well, I thought, if they're such fools I'll get ahead of them and teach them a lesson. One ill turn deserves another. It would have been a sharper lesson if you'd given me a little more time and more Men. Still I have done much that you will find it hard to mend or undo in your lives. And it will be pleasant to think of that and set it against my injuries."[13]

Saruman's petty malice is contrasted here with Frodo's forgiveness and generosity. When Saruman tries to stab him and fails because of Frodo's mail shirt, Sam draws his sword.

"No, Sam," said Frodo. "Do not kill him even now. For he has not hurt me. And in any case I do not wish him to be slain in this evil mood. He was great once, of a noble kind we should not dare to raise our hands against. He is fallen, and his cure is beyond us: but I would still spare him, in the hope that he may find it."[14]

It is worth noting that the virtues exhibited by Frodo here and elsewhere are more the traditional "feminine" virtues, such as compassion, concern for people and relationships, supportiveness, rather than "masculine" traits, such as aggressiveness, desire to win, refusal to be dependent. Frodo shows compassion to Gollum as well as Saruman, concern and supportiveness for Sam, Bilbo, and the other Hobbits. On his return to the Shire, he takes little part in the fighting necessary to undo Saruman's evil work and forbids Merry and Pippin to kill any Hobbit, even if they have been evildoers. "There is to be no slaying of hobbits even if they have gone over to the other side. . . . No hobbit has ever killed another hobbit on purpose in the Shire and it is not to begin now."[15]

Merry and Pippin respect Frodo's authority, but it is a moral authority, based on his sacrifices. To the Hobbits of the Shire, it is Merry and Pippin who seem the heroes.

Frodo dropped quietly out of all the doings of the Shire, and Sam was pained to notice how little honor he had in his own country. Few people knew or wanted to know about his deeds and adventures: their admiration was given mostly to Mr. Meriodoc and Mr. Peregrin and (if Sam had known it) to himself.[16]

As we saw earlier, Tolkien said several times that Sam Gamgee is in some sense the "chief hero" of *The Lord of the Rings.* Since Sam is a somewhat comic character at the beginning of the story and Frodo's servant throughout the story, this is somewhat surprising. Surely Sam, though an important character in the book, is only a secondary character, the servant. But as Chesterton says about Saint Francis, "He found his vocation in being the secondary character, the servant."[17] Sam starts out as comic and somewhat childish but steadily grows and develops, until at the end of the book he has so grown in stature that we are not surprised to see the book end with his return to his wife and family after saying farewell to Frodo at the Grey Havens.

There have been other books in which a "comic relief" servant becomes a deeper character by the end of the story. In *The Pickwick Papers,* Sam Weller undergoes this kind of transformation, and in *Don Quixote,* Sancho Panza to some extent does the same. But by and large, the comic servant remains comic and remains a servant, though he may have serious moments and sometimes act independently.

At the end of *The Lord of the Rings,* however, Frodo tells Sam:

"You are my heir: all that I had and might have had I leave to you . . . your hands and your wits will be needed everywhere. You will be the Mayor, of course, as long as you want to be, and the most famous gardener in history; and you will . . . keep alive the memory of the age that is gone, so that people willremembertheGreatDangerandsolovetheirbelovedlandallthemore."[18]

Since the Mayor of the Shire is the chief office among the Hobbits, this is as if Sam Weller were to become prime minister at the end of *The Pickwick Papers* or Sancho Panza become in truth and not in jest the ruler of a province at the end of *Don Quixote.* It is not merely the social realities of eighteenth-century England or seventeenth-century Spain that make these events impossible in *Pickwick* or *Quixote;* neither Sam Weller nor Sancho Panza has reached a stature that would make even a more modest elevation—for instance, moving into their master's place in society—plausible.

How does Tolkien make Sam's growth in stature convincing? He starts off by giving Sam more independent judgment than the usual servant of fiction: Sam conspires with Merry and Pippin for the good of Frodo, reporting Frodo's plans to them so they can help him in his quest and not let him slip away from the Shire on his own. Also Tolkien gives Sam the very important characteristic of openness to new ideas and experiences; he longs to meet the Elves and dreams of one day seeing an elephant. In this, Sam is considerably different from the usual inhabitant of the Shire, and even from Bilbo when we first meet him. Most Hobbits are bourgeois and rather smug, not interested in anything beyond the Shire and suspicious of anything unusual or "unhobbitlike."

In what sense, then, is Sam "the real Hobbit, the successor to Bilbo in the first book," as Tolkien says in the letter quoted earlier? In another letter, Tolkien fills in with this somewhat cryptic comment:

Sam is meant to be lovable and laughable. Some readers he irritates and even infuriates. I can well understand it. All hobbits at times affect me in the same way, though I remain very fond of them. But Sam can be very "trying." He is a more representative hobbit than any others we have to see much of; and he has consequently a stronger ingredient of that quality which even some hobbits found at times hard to bear: a vulgarity—by which I do not mean a mere "down-to-earthness"—a mental myopia which is proud of itself, a smugness (in varying degrees) and cocksureness, and a readiness to measure and sum up all things from a limited experience, largely enshrined in a sententious traditional "wisdom." We only meet exceptional hobbits in close companionship—those who had a grace or gift: a vision of beauty, and a reverence for things nobler than themselves, at war with their rustic self-satisfaction. Imagine Sam without his education by Bilbo and his fascination with things elvish![19]

So Sam's difference from other Hobbits consists of "a vision of beauty, and a reverence for things nobler than [himself]." This is very much in line with Tolkien's description of the "structure" of his work: "primarily a study of the ennoblement (or sanctification) of the humble."[20]

The pattern of development of character we have found in Bilbo and Frodo is repeated in Sam. He starts out as a dependent, childlike character and gradually takes more and more responsibility. Up until the time Frodo leaves the rest of the Fellowship to make his way to Mount Doom alone to destroy the Ring, both he and Sam are protected and guided by Gandalf and Aragorn. When Frodo tries to go on alone,

Sam is aware of how Frodo is thinking and insists on going with him. As they journey across the wild lands on the border of the Dark Lord's kingdom, Sam deals with the practical aspects of their journey, such as food. He attempts to shield Frodo from harm, not always wisely. When Frodo decides that they must descend a cliff to continue their journey, Sam tries to go first.

"Very good," said Sam gloomily, "but I'm going first."

"You?" said Frodo. "What's made you change your mind about climbing?"

"I haven't changed my mind. But it's only sense: put the one lowest as is most likely to slip. I don't want to come down atop of you and knock you off—no sense in killing two with one fall."

Before Frodo could stop him he sat down, swung his legs over the brink and twisted around, scrabbling with his toes for a foothold. It is doubtful if he ever did anything braver in cold blood, or more unwise.[21]

Frodo hauls him back, and they find their way down, helped by a rope Sam has brought, with Frodo in the lead. But Sam's rash attempt, like Bilbo's adventure with the Trolls, marks a development in his character. He has done something brave, and done it to help someone else. It marks the beginning of a new stage of growth.

When Frodo allows Gollum to join their party as a guide, Sam is both suspicious and jealous. He fears that Gollum will betray Frodo and is also possessive of Frodo and jealous of Gollum's growing love for Frodo. As Tolkien says in a letter:

Sam was cocksure, and deep down a little conceited, but his conceit had been transformed by his devotion to Frodo. He did not think of himself as heroic, or even brave, or in any way admirable—except in his service and loyalty to his master. This had an ingredient (probably inevitable) of pride and posses- siveness: it is difficult to exclude it from the devotion of those who perform such service. In any case it prevented him from fully understanding the master he loved and from following him in his gradual education to the nobility of service to the unlovable and of perception of damaged good in the corrupt. . . . If he had understood better what was going on between Frodo and Gollum things might have turned out differently in the end. For me perhaps the most poignant moment in the tale comes . . . when Sam fails to notice the complete change in Gollum's tone and aspect. "Nothing, nothing," said Gollum softly. "Nice master." His repentance is blighted and all Frodo's pity is (in a sense) wasted.[22]

Sam realizes his own limitations; he sees Frodo as being beyond his comprehension: "I hope the master will think it out carefully. He's as wise as any, but he's soft-hearted, that's what he is. It's beyond any Gamgee to guess what he'll do next."[23] But in practical terms he grows more and more protective of Frodo. When he and Frodo are taken into custody by Men of Gondor who patrol the borders of Sauron's kingdom, Sam stays awake while Frodo sleeps for fear of treachery by "all these great Men about."[24]

In answering the questions of the leader of the patrol, Faramir, the younger son of Denethor, Sam gives away information about the Ring, rather as Bilbo did at Bree. But he stands up to Faramir and earns respect both for his faithfulness and for his shrewdness. Sam's virtues throughout are "peasant" virtues; his mind is described as "slow but shrewd," he is faithful, persevering, undaunted. Frodo becomes almost a saint; Sam does not. Merry and Pippin become heroes in battle; Sam does not earn that sort of glory. But he does acquire the virtue and the wisdom he needs to eventually become the leader and ruler of the Hobbits—the Mayor of the Shire. Had he become less of a Hobbit he would be less fitted for that job, a job that Frodo, and even Merry and Pippin, have grown too great for.

After Sam has innocently "aborted" Gollum's incipient repentance, Gollum reverts to his original plan of leading Sam and Frodo into the lair of the giant spider, Shelob. Sam escapes unharmed, and the spider is terribly wounded, but Frodo is stung by Shelob and put into a deathlike trance by her venom. Sam, believing that Frodo is dead, feels that it is his duty to carry on Frodo's quest: he takes the Ring and Frodo's sword, determined to complete the quest by destroying the Ring in the fires of Crack of Doom as Frodo planned to do. That a giant spider is involved and that Frodo is only drugged into unconsciousness and is eventually rescued by Sam remind us forcibly of Bilbo's earlier struggle with the giant spiders of Mirkwood.

Like Bilbo in a similar situation, Sam has no real thought of running away and leaving the spider's prey. As soon as he realizes that Frodo is alive, Sam bends every effort toward rescue and, with the aid of the Ring and Bilbo's sword, does manage to rescue Frodo, as Bilbo rescued the Dwarves with the same Ring and sword.

Like the other Hobbits who have worn the Ring (Sméagol-Gollum, Bilbo, and Frodo) Sam feels the temptation to use the power of the Ring himself. The Ring insinuates into Sam's mind the image of himself as

Samwise the Strong, Hero of the Age, striding with flaming sword across the darkened land, and armies flocking to his call as he marched to the overthrow of Bared-dûr. And then all the clouds rolled away and the white sun shone, and at his command the vale of Gorgorath became a garden of trees and brought forth fruit. He had only to put on the Ring and claim it for his own and all this could be.

In that hour of trial it was the love of his master that helped most to hold him firm; but also deep down in him lived still unconquered plain hobbit-sense: he knew in the core of his heart he was not large enough to bear such a burden, even if such visions were not a mere cheat to betray him. The one small garden of a free gardener was all his need and due, not a garden swollen to a realm; his own lands to use, not the lands of others to command.

"And anyway all those notions are only a trick," he said to himself.[25]

Here again, just as humility and love have saved Bilbo on previous occasions, they save Sam now. He overcomes the temptation, spares Frodo, and has the strength to give Frodo back the Ring, despite the hold it develops on each of its wearers. As they go on into the land of the Dark Lord, Sam increasingly has to support and help Frodo, until it is almost he who is the leader; Frodo is the Ring-bearer, but Sam "carries" Frodo, psychologically, emotionally, and toward the end, literally.

As we noticed earlier with Frodo himself, Sam's virtues are more the traditional "feminine" virtues than the traditional "masculine" ones. He exhibits concrete wisdom rather than abstract reasoning, finds relationships more important than objects, is supportive, nurturing, and self-sacrificing. His concern with getting Frodo to eat good meals and keeping him warm and comfortable is a "wifely" or "motherly" concern. He is content to step back and let Frodo take the leadership role. Even his jealousy of Gollum is a traditionally "feminine" trait based on possessiveness toward Frodo. There are scenes where he expresses his love for Frodo tenderly, as in one case where Frodo is sleeping, and there seems to be a light, almost a halo, about his careworn face: "He shook his head, as if finding words useless, and murmured 'I love him. He's like that and sometimes it shines through somehow. But I love him, whether or no.' "[26]

Some feminists might argue that these "feminine" virtues are not exclusively feminine and are perhaps not even virtues at all. Tolkien would agree with the first point—after all he has given these virtues to Sam—but not the second. For a Christian, the sacrifice of self for others is the height of virtue: "Greater love has no man than this, that he lay down his life for his friend." Men have certainly exploited these virtues in women, but that does not mean that they are not virtues. In fact, it may even be that it is men more than women who need to learn these virtues and that women must counter learned or natural tendencies and be more self-confident and self-assertive. But for Christians, Christ himself is the supreme model, and Christ was the man who laid down his life for others.

Sam's faithful service to Frodo and his eventual rise to Mayor of the Shire can be taken as an illustration of the saying of Christ "He who would be greatest among you must be least, and a servant."

Tolkien was fond of Chesterton's poem *The Ballad of the White Horse,* though he came to be dissatisfied with it in some ways. In writing about Sam, he might have had in the back of his mind the words of King Alfred in the poem.

> And well may God with the serving-folk
> Cast in His dreadful lot
> For was He not a servant
> And was He not forgot?[27]

W. H. Auden, who was an admirer of Tolkien's work, has written insightfully about the way in which the metaphor of servant and master can be used to illuminate the nature of the self.

The relation between Master and Servant is not given by nature or Fate, but comes into being through an act of conscious volition. . . . A dialogue requires two voices, but if it is the inner dialogue of human personality that is to be expressed artistically, the two characters employed to express it and the relationship must be of a special kind. The pair must in certain respects be similar i.e. they must be of the same sex, and in others, physical and tempermental, polar opposites . . . and they must be inseparable i.e. the relationship between them must be of a kind which is not affected by the passage of time or the fluctuations of mood and which makes it plausible that wherever one of them is, whatever he is doing, the other should be here too. There is only one relationship which satisfies all these conditions, that between master and personal servant.[28]

Auden cites as examples the two great comic servants of literature mentioned above, Sam Weller and Sancho Panza. If we look at Frodo and Sam from this angle, we can see that they can be thought of as two aspects of one personality. Sam is Frodo's more "Hobbit-like" side, shrewd but limited, distrustful of things outside his experience.

Frodo, on the other hand, is a Hobbit raised to heights of nobility, a Hobbit "saint." Though it is true that Sam does not reach these heights, there is something in him that responds to Frodo's nobility. Like Frodo, he spares Gollum when he could have killed him.

It would be just to slay this treacherous, murderous, creature, just and many times deserved: and also it seemed the only safe thing to do. But deep in his heart there was something that restrained him: he could not strike this wretched thing lying in the dust, forlorn, ruinous, utterly wretched. He himself, though only for a little while, had borne the Ring and now dimly he guessed the agony of Gollum's shrivelled mind and body, enslaved to that Ring, unable to find peace or relief ever in life again.[29]

At this moment, Sam rises nearly to the height Frodo has risen to, the ability to see "the nobility of service to the unlovable, and of perception of damaged good in the corrupt." Thus Frodo is Sam's nobler side, just as Sam is Frodo's earthy Hobbit side. The two together make one whole person, or perhaps more truly Frodo, Sam, Merry, and Pippin make one whole person.

And this is a human person, not a Hobbit. For just as the Elves represent one side of human nature, the Hobbits represent another. The

Elves are the artistic, scientific part of humanity, the Hobbits are the home-loving, family-loving, comfort-loving part of human nature. Sam the "real Hobbit" marries his childhood sweetheart and lives a long and happy life in the Shire, while Frodo can no longer find peace there and must go on to the Undying Land across the sea. But just as *The Lord of the Rings* began in the jolly, happy, comfortable world of the Hobbits, it ends there. The last words of the story are:

Sam turned to Bywater and so came back up the Hill as day was ending once more. And he went on and there was yellow light and fire within; and the evening meal was ready, and he was expected. And Rose drew him in and set him in his chair, and put little Elanor upon his lap.

He drew a deep breath. "Well, I'm back," he said.[30]

6. Elves and Others

We saw in the last chapter that the Hobbits represent one side of human nature, the Elves another. It is time to see what morals Tolkien intends us to draw from his picture of the artistic and scientific side of human nature as isolated and transfigured in the Elves. The Elves are akin to the scientist in that they love the beauty of the world and seek to understand it, akin to the artist in that they are "subcreators," embellishing the world with what mortals call magic but which Tolkien hints is a sort of fiction, in fact, a sort of fiction rather like that which Tolkien himself produces.

It is obvious enough that those who love the world run the risk of not looking beyond the world, and indeed, the particular "doom" or "fate" of the Elves is to be "bound to the circles of the world" until its end. Tolkien pictures them as sometimes envious of human beings because at death humans are free of "the circles of the world." Humans envy the Elves their immortality; Elves envy humans their mortality.

But the chief moral failing of the Elves as pictured by Tolkien is what Tolkien rather obscurely calls "embalming." This consists of trying to hold on to the past, trying to resist change.

Mere *change* as such is not represented as evil: it is the unfolding of the story and to refuse this is of course against the design of God. But the elvish weakness is in these terms naturally to regret the past, and become unwilling to face change: as if a man were to hate a very long book still going on, and wished to settle down in a favorite chapter. Hence they fell in a measure to Sauron's deceits: they desired some "power" over things as they are . . . to make their particular will to preservation effective: to arrest change and keep things always fresh and fair.[1]

This Elvish failing is certainly one with implications for us ordinary mortals. We experience happiness at some time or place or in some circumstance, and we then try to repeat or preserve the experience that made us happy. Men and women attempt to hold on to their youth or to hold on to some experience such as *falling* in love, which is only a stage in a process, one that should develop into further stages.

Broadly speaking, such "holding on" seems to be a form of greed or avarice. In its simplest form, avarice is the desire for money or property, and interestingly enough, in *The Hobbit* we see the King of the Wood-elves pictured as perhaps somewhat desiring the dragon's treasure and certainly highly possessive of his own lands and jealous of any intrusion on them. More generally, money in our society can be and often is used to resist change. The rich man or woman may try to stay young, to be secure against outside influences in various ways. The rich often tend to insulate themselves from the rest of the world and to pursue an unvarying round of social activities.

Money, property, power, influence are all ways of "taking charge" of the world, of making things go our way. Tolkien's friend C. S. Lewis explored this idea in his novel *Perelandra*,[2] which, incidentally, was one of the books Lewis read to the group of friends called the Inklings, of which Tolkien was a member. Lewis, in *Perelandra*, embodied in fictional form the idea that, though we should give ourselves up to the will of God, we in our society use money and property to ensure that our will and not God's is done and to avoid new experiences that God might send us to help us grow and develop.

In Tolkien's work we see this resistance to change, this form of possessiveness, pictured in different ways. We have already seen Denethor's resistance to change ("I would have things as they were in all the days of my life . . ."), and Denethor belongs to an ancient human lineage with Elvish blood. The Dwarves are pictured as avaricious in an obvious, material way, greedy for treasure. The "less advanced" or "lower" groups of Elves are possessive about territory, like the King of the Wood-elves who tells the Dwarves, "It is a crime to wander in my realm without leave. Do you forget you were in my kingdom, using the road my people made?"[3]

In the legends hinted at in *The Lord of the Rings* and developed more fully in *The Silmarillion*, Fëanor, one of the greatest of the Elves, creates marvelous jewels that contain some of the power of the Two Trees, which are later destroyed by Melkor, the first Dark Lord,

Sauron's predecessor. A good deal of the harm done by Melkor could be healed if Fëanor would give up his creations to be used for the common good, but he refuses. In fact, he is so possessive of the jewels that he flees from his homeland because he fears that pressure might be put on him to give them up.

Later in the history of the Elves in Middle-earth, we see Elvish kings trying to isolate their kingdoms, shut them off from the outside world, suspicious even of Elves who come into their kingdom from other Elvish realms. In *The Lord of the Rings* we see a similar suspicion on the part of the Elves of Lothlórien, who insist on blindfolding Gimli the Dwarf lest he learn the secrets of their kingdom when he is being led to their Lord and Lady.

We have spoken of Elvish possessiveness and resistance to change as a form of avarice; it might be worthwhile to look at the other traditional "deadly sins": pride, envy, sloth, anger, gluttony, and lust. We are sometimes shown pride, anger, and perhaps envy in Elves or Men of Elvish lineage, but never sloth or gluttony (with one dubious exception in the case of the Wood-elves in *The Hobbit*[4]). Hobbits can exhibit sloth or gluttony, as in the case of "Fatty" Bolger early in *The Fellowship of the Ring*. None of the characters, Elf or Dwarf, human or Hobbit, shows anything that might be described as lust; the whole area of sexual desire is largely left out of Tolkien's work. This puts it into sharp contrast with most modern literature, which seems obsessed with sex in almost any form.

Those who have parodied or imitated Tolkien have often tried to graft sexual themes onto a Tolkienian or pseudo-Tolkienian world (as for instance the Harvard Lampoon parody *Bored of the Rings*[5] published at the height of the 1960s craze for Tolkien's work). Whether because of lack of skill or because of something in the nature of the epic world depicted by Tolkien, these attempts always seem to fail: the sexual themes seem incongruous and obtrusive.

It can be argued, of course, that sex is an important part of life and that a fully developed picture of people and relationships should include it. But that does not mean it is obligatory to include sexual themes in every kind of story. However, this does raise the question of Tolkien's treatment of women, and of love between men and women.

Tolkien gives some attention, at places where he finds it appropriate, to romantic love. We have the heroic love of Aragorn for Arwen, daughter of Elrond, and the homely, domestic love of Sam Gamgee and Rosie Cotten. Somewhere in between is the love story of Éowyn, daughter of King Théoden. She begins with a romantic, unrealistic love for Aragorn, who has loved Arwen for centuries (he is of long-lived human-Elvish stock, and Arwen can choose either Elvish immortality or mortality with her human lover). Eventually Éowyn finds happiness with Faramir, son of Denethor.

Tolkien would agree that these stories take up little space in the trilogy, but he would deny that they are unimportant. As he says in a letter:

Since we now try to deal with "ordinary life" springing up ever unquenched under the trample of world policies and events, there are love-stories touched in, or love in different modes, wholly absent from *The Hobbit.* But the highest love-story, that of Aragorn and Arwen, Elrond's daughter, is only alluded to as a known thing . . . I think the simple "rustic" love of Sam and his Rosie (nowhere elaborated) is *absolutely essential* to the studies of his (the chief hero's) character, and to the theme of the relation of ordinary life (breathing, eating, working, begetting) and quests, sacrifice, causes, and the "longing for Elves," and sheer beauty.[6]

Thus we can see that there are several elements that Tolkien tries to include in his stories:

1. ordinary life ("breathing, eating, working, begetting")
2. the heroic ("quests, sacrifice, causes")
3. the "magical" (" 'longing for Elves,' and sheer beauty")

Most of *The Hobbit* and most of *The Lord of the Rings* are concerned with the second category, the heroic. The first category, ordinary life, is used in *The Hobbit* as a frame for the story, which begins and ends in the comfortable domesticity of Bilbo's hobbit-hole. *The Lord of the Rings* begins with Bilbo and Frodo's combined birthday party and ends with Sam's return to his family: it, too, is framed by scenes of "ordinary life." But since it is a richer and more complex work than *The Hobbit,* it contains more depth of ordinary life—love and friendship as well as food and comfort at home. There are also more scenes of "ordinary life" interspersed in the story, to contrast with the heroic element.

These include things as diverse as the home life of Tom Bombadil and his Goldberry, the simple meal of herbs and stewed rabbit that gives a title to one of the chapters in *The Two Towers,* and the love story of Éowyn. Each of these parts of "ordinary life" is threatened by the Dark Lord. Gandalf says of Tom Bombadil: "In the end if all else is conquered, Bombadil will fall."[7] The land of Ithilien where Sam and Frodo have their meal is "a land already less barren and ruinous" than other lands they have traveled. "It seemed good to be reprieved, to walk in a land which had only been for a few years under the domination of the Dark Lord and was not yet wholly fallen into decay."[8] But if Sauron were able to consolidate his rule over this still-beautiful land, it would become as dark and polluted as his central kingdom of Mordor.

Éowyn's final, happy love comes to her after the defeat of Sauron, but her earlier, unhappy love for Aragorn is played out against the background of Sauron's intrigues against her father's kingdom and Aragorn's battles against the Dark Lord's forces. As Faramir tells her:

"You desired to have the love of the Lord Aragorn. Because he was high and puissant, and you wished to have renown and glory and be lifted above the mean things that crawl on the earth. And as a great captain may to a young soldier he seemed to you admirable. For so he is, a lord among men, the greatest that now is. But when he gave you only understanding and pity, you desired to have nothing, unless a brave death in battle."[9]

Éowyn has here the same option that Denethor had and took, that her father had and refused: the option to cling to her mistake and refuse to open herself up to a new opportunity. Éowyn, like her father, has the courage to change, to accept the truth in Faramir's words and the love he offers. Despite its brevity, Éowyn's story is one of considerable depth and poignancy.

It is, of course, brief, only an interlude in the wider story of the War of the Ring. But *The Lord of the Rings* is, as a whole, a story of the heroic, of "quests, sacrifice, causes." The defense of ordinary life is the motive for the heroic; the enjoyment of ordinary life is the reward of the heroic. Aragorn and his Rangers have spent long years defending the Shire and other civilized and peaceful lands from the threats of evil. As Aragorn says at the Council of Elrond:

"Lonely men are we, Rangers of the wild, hunters—but hunters ever of the servants of the Enemy; for they are found in many places. . . . Peace and freedom, do you say? The North would have known them little but for us. Fear would have destroyed them. But when dark things come from the houseless hills, or creep from sunless woods, they fly from us. What roads would any dare to tread, what safety would there be in quiet lands, or the homes of simple men at night . . . if [they] were not guarded ceaselessly. Yet we would not have it otherwise. If simple folk are free from care and fear, simple they will be, and we must be secret to keep them so. That has been the task of my kindred, while the years have lengthened and the grass has grown."[10]

We see in the last book of the trilogy that Aragorn has his reward: he marries Arwen and at long last takes the throne of his fathers, to reign in power and peace. Frodo, on the other hand, can find no peace in the peaceful Shire after the defeat of the Enemy. As he tells Sam, "I have been too deeply hurt, Sam. I tried to save the Shire, and it has been saved, but not for me. It must often be so, Sam, when things are in danger: someone has to give them up, lose them so that others may keep them."[11]

Frodo's reward is to go with the Elves to the Undying Lands across the Western Sea. Tolkien says in a letter that Bilbo and Frodo will not be immortal: their lives will be prolonged but not unending.

Frodo was sent or allowed to pass over Sea to heal him—if that could be done *before* he died. He would eventually have to "pass away": no mortal could or can abide for ever on Earth, or within Time. So he went both to a purgatory and to a reward, for a while: a period of reflection and peace and a gaining of a truer understanding of his position in littleness and in greatness, spent still in Time amid the natural beauty of "Arda Unmarred" the Earth unspoiled by Evil.[12]

It may very well be that in the back of Tolkien's mind was a distinctively Catholic idea of different "vocations" or ways of life to which we are called by God. Ordinary laypeople are called on to make sacrifices for their religion, but they will usually find their rewards in family life, in the "ordinary life" that Tolkien speaks of. But the celibate priest, or the monk or nun, give up these good things of ordinary life and find their reward in service ("I tried to save the Shire, and it was saved") and in the hope of heaven. Recently, Catholic theologians have extended the idea of "vocation" to any task that God may ask of a man or woman in this life. But for an older Catholic like Tolkien, "vocation" would usually mean a vocation to the priesthood or the "religious" life of a monk or nun. We might remember that in a letter quoted earlier Tolkien said of Frodo, "He has a vocation, as it were." Frodo's refusal to take up arms during the Scouring of the Shire is another hint in this direction.

"Ordinary life" is contrasted, on the one hand, with the heroic life ("heroic virtue" is a term used in Catholic writing about the saints). On the other hand, it is contrasted with the "magical" or "Elvish." The comfortably self-satisfied "bourgeois" mind (like that of the ordinary Hobbit) is as little likely to explore this dimension of life as it is to explore the heroic dimension. As I said at the beginning of this chapter, the Elves are to some extent representatives of both the scientist and the artist. The scholar or scientist—the person who wants to know "the truth of things" more than anything else, departs from bourgeois ordinariness in one way; the writer or artist departs from it in another. As an academic and a writer, I have encountered both attitudes, and Tolkien certainly did as well.

In fact, those who are both professors and popular writers, as Tolkien was (and as I am), sometimes find themselves in a sort of double bind, distrusted by writers because they are academics and envied by academic colleagues for their popular success. The more prestigious the university and the greater the success, the stronger this double bind becomes. Both Tolkien and his friend Lewis found themselves criticized by their Oxford colleagues out of thinly veiled envy, as have other Oxford dons who have dabbled successfully in fiction (J. I. M. Stewart, for instance, whose successful detective stories are written under the pseudonym "Michael Innes").

This distrust of the scholar or artist by the ordinary person is given literary form in Tolkien's work by the attitudes of many ordinary folk to the Elves. Hobbits in general are suspicious of Elves and anything to do with Elves: Bilbo, Sam, and Frodo all come in for criticism because of dealing with the Elves. The Men of Gondor, including Boromir and some of Faramir's men, have a distrust of Elves and a willingness to believe unpleasant stories about them that is reminiscent to some extent of racial prejudice in our mundane world (prejudice against Jews or Asians, especially, often contains a shrillness based on an unacknowledged fear of the intellectual superiority believed to characterize them).

Envy, properly speaking, is a desire that no one excel the envious person, so envy will desire the destruction of the feared superior even if that results in no other advantage to the envious person. The envious poor man might like to be rich, for example, but even if he cannot be rich would prefer that no one be richer than himself (I use the masculine form here deliberately: I think envy is far more a vice of males than of females).

The only character in *The Lord of the Rings* to embody envy is Saruman: as we have seen, he is willing to go to a great deal of trouble to destroy the happiness and peace of the Shire, even though he knows that this will do him no good in the long run. At one point when he is trying to "con" Gandalf into co-operating with him, he uses a phrase very characteristic of envy, "In time, no one will stand higher . . ." (he says "than ourselves" but means "than myself"). That no one should "stand higher" is the dream of envy: some forms of egalitarianism are fed by envy, by men content to be equal if no one is superior to them. (Again I say "men" advisedly: women have related vices, such as jealousy, but rarely this one.)

Insofar as one can judge a man's character from the outside, from accounts of him by others, it seems not unlikely that Tolkien himself had some inclination to possessiveness and envy. But artists are fortunate in having as a fringe benefit of their profession the ability to *use* the sins they are most prone to, objectifying them in their villains and thus becoming somewhat more aware of the real unpleasantness of those vices. Niggle is to some extent a self-portrait, with more humility than charity to self, featuring what Tolkien saw as some of his own weaknesses, such as procrastination.

Most writers will tell you that it is easier to write convincing villains than convincing heroes: to depict a villain we have merely to exaggerate our own vices. To write a convincing character better than ourselves requires both more imagination and more humility: often the hero, especially of first novels, is a flattering and decidedly unhumble self-portrait of the author, and these self-indulgent characterizations can seem far from admirable to the critical outsider.

In fact, writers about writing have speculated that all of a good novelist's characters are in some sense reflections of his or her own personality, people the novelist might conceivably have become. This means that, for a woman to write convincing male characters, she must be in touch with the masculine elements of her own character, and for a man to write convincing female characters, he must be in touch with the feminine elements in his own character. The bad novelist, of course, avoids the problem by writing stereotyped characters based secondhand on the writings of better authors.

Tolkien was, I think, in contact with the feminine elements of his own makeup but, partly because of his upbringing and the society he lived in, was more able to give these elements embodiment in male characters such as Sam and Frodo than to use these elements in creating major female characters.

There is one successful and powerful female character in *The Lord of the Rings,* Galadriel the Lady of Lórien. She is beautiful enough to cause awestruck adoration in Gimli, the Dwarf, whose people are traditionally suspicious of the Elves. She is powerful enough to be the bearer of one of the three Rings of Power belonging to the Elves. She is the only Elvish character to show great mastery of what non-Elves would call "magic" (though she herself questions the term). At the same time, Galadriel exhibits traditional "feminine" characteristics: gentleness, understanding of personal relationships, compassion. In Galadriel's mirror, Frodo and Sam each find an understanding of themselves through what they choose to ask to see.

Galadriel's descriptions of herself are interesting. On first meeting

Frodo and his companions, she says, "I will not give you counsel, saying do this, or do that. For not in doing or contriving nor in choosing between this course and another can I avail: but only in knowing what was and is, and in part also what shall be."[13] Of course, this does not mean that she cannot decide or plan on her own behalf, only that it is not her task (though perhaps it is sometimes Gandalf's) to decide or plan *for others*.

What she does do is hold up or show the alternatives to each member of the Fellowship: Sam describes his own experience thus: "She seemed to be looking inside me and asking me what I would do if she gave me a chance of flying back home to the Shire to a nice little hole with —with a bit of garden of my own."[14] (As Sam's hesitation shows, reunion with Rosie Cotten is probably part of the temptation.) Each member of the Company feels he is being offered a choice; only Boromir, who is soon to yield to a real temptation, feels that this is something that Galadriel is actively doing—that she is tempting them, trying to influence them. The others realize, even if somewhat dimly, that what she has done is show them "what is and what may be"; she has made their choices explicit and concrete.

When she gives Sam and Frodo a chance to look in her "mirror" (a magical pool that shows visions of what is or might be), Sam makes a natural choice—to know what is going on at home. He sees the spoiling of the Shire by Saruman's meddling, which disturbs his peace and perhaps has other bad effects. (His impatience with Gollum, for example, may be partly due to the worries aroused here.)

Frodo lets the "mirror" tell him what it wills, but lacks skill to interpret it. Reading the scene with knowledge of the book, we see that several key future events are shown to him (Gandalf's "resurrection," an enemy ship captured by Aragorn, perhaps his own departure over the Sea). But then he sees the Eye of Sauron searching for him; he is afraid, but Galadriel reassures him.

"Do not be afraid! But do not think that only by singing amid the trees, nor even by the slender arrows of elven-bows is this land of Lothlórien maintained and defended against its Enemy. I say to you, Frodo, that even as I speak to you, I perceive the Dark Lord and know his mind, or all of his mind that concerns the Elves. As he gropes ever to see me and my thought. But still the door is closed."[15]

We see from this that Galadriel has won a battle that Denethor is later to lose: the battle to know the mind of the Dark Lord without being bent to his evil. The fact that she is able to do this shows that she is one of the most powerful beings on the side of good.

Impressed by her power, Frodo freely offers the Ring to her. By simply accepting this offer she could become the new Ring-wielder, rally the forces of good, and defeat Sauron. But as we have seen, the Ring is not just power, but evil power, and the power to dominate, to manage others' wills. She herself knows the consequences of accepting this offer, knows her own weaknesses.

"I do not deny that my heart has greatly desired to ask what you offer. For many long years I have pondered what I might do, should the Great Ring came into my hands. . . . And now at last it comes. You will give me the Ring freely! In place of the Dark Lord you will set up a Queen. And I shall not be dark, but beautiful and terrible as the Morning and the Night! Fair as the Sea and the Sun and the Snow upon the Mountain! Dreadful as the Storm and the Lightning! Stronger than the foundations of the earth. All shall love me and despair!"

She lifted up her hand and from the ring that she wore there issued a great light that illumined her alone and left all else dark. She stood before Frodo seeming now tall beyond measurement, and beautiful beyond enduring, terrible and worshipful. Then she let her hand fall, and the light faded, and suddenly she laughed again, and lo! she was shrunken: a slender elf-woman, clad in simple white, whose gentle voice was soft and sad.

"I pass the test," she said. "I will diminish, and go into the West, and remain Galadriel."[16]

Every detail of this important scene is significant. Tolkien pictures Galadriel's temptation as the temptation to be universally, irresistibly, loved. Her metaphors for her own beauty are all taken from nature. The light the ring sheds is *only* on her, "leaving all else in darkness." Envy, the desire to be pre-eminent, is a traditional masculine vice; jealousy, the desire to be loved uniquely and exclusively, is a traditional

feminine vice. Galadriel imagines herself the focus of everyone's possessive love; since she cannot belong to everyone, "all will love me, and
despair!"

The words in which Galadriel refuses the temptation are both beautiful and significant: "I will diminish . . . "; she can face losing power,
becoming less than she is, as Denethor or Saruman could not. Next,
"and go into the West"; she will leave the Middle-earth she loves, give
up her fight to preserve an Elvish remnant in Middle-earth. Finally,
"and remain Galadriel"; she will retain her true self, be her own woman
and not the tool of the evil power in the Ring.

Galadriel knows that the power of the Ring would corrupt her, and
she cannot be tempted, as some good and loving people might be, by
the temptation to do good for others by evil means. Sam tells her he
wishes that she had accepted the Ring.

"You'd put things to rights. . . . You'd make some folk pay for their dirty
work."

"I would," she said. "That is how it would begin. But it would not stop
with that, alas!"[17]

In Lewis's *Perelandra,* an evil power tempts a woman in precisely this
way, by the temptation to do good to others by means that she knows
to be evil. But, as Galadriel knows, "it would not stop with that." Evil
means corrupt good ends, a truth forgotten by those who try to achieve
justice or liberation by terrorism and the death of the innocent.

About Galadriel, Tolkien makes an interesting comment in a letter:

I think it is true that I owe much of this character to Catholic teaching and
imagination about Mary, but actually Galadriel was a penitent: in her youth
a leader in the rebellion against the Valar (the angelic guardians). At the end
of the First Age she proudly refused forgiveness or permission to return. She
was pardoned because of her resistance to the final and overwhelming temptation to take the Ring for herself.[18]

Galadriel is like Mary, the mother of Christ, in her humility, her
willingness to be a humble "handmaid of the Lord" rather than trying
to be Queen. As with Mary, humility receives its reward: "The one

who humbles himself shall be exalted." But Galadriel is unlike Mary in having previously refused to learn this lesson and in having to repent and relearn.

The final important character whose virtues and vices we will consider in this chapter is Gandalf. As a wizard, he is an angelic being embodied in human form and sent to help in the battle of good against evil. This is a mission with its dangers; Saruman, who is in the same position, falls victim to temptation and becomes evil. Very early in the story Gandalf is offered the Ring by Frodo and refuses it for the same reasons as Galadriel:

"No!" cried Gandalf, springing to his feet, "with that power I should have power too great and terrible. And over me the Ring would gain a power still greater and more deadly." His eyes flashed and his face was lit as by a fire within. "Do not tempt me! For I do not wish to become like the Dark Lord himself. Yet the way of the Ring to my heart is by pity, pity for weakness and the desire of strength to do good."[19]

Gandalf's temptation, to which we shall return, is the desire to *make* those he is sent to help be "good" in *his* way. As Tolkien says in an unfinished draft for a letter:

Gandalf as Ring-Lord would have been far worse than Sauron. He would have remained "righteous," but self-righteous . . . Gandalf would have made good detestable and seem evil.[20]

Gandalf resists the temptation, but he is not perfect. He is sometimes impatient and even slightly arrogant; like an adult dealing with recalcitrant children, he is sometimes tempted to do things himself or insist that things be done *his* way instead of letting those in his charge learn and grow.

We have already seen that he usually resists this temptation: in his dealings with Bilbo and Frodo we have seen him getting out of the way to let them develop on their own. But the temptation is perennial for all those who seek to teach, to help others by such wisdom as they have. It is the temptation to tell rather than to let the students learn, to impose your vision instead of letting them find their own. But, as Gandalf knows, this is one form of the urge to dominate, to rule: the teacher, the wise one, who gives in to it is no longer a teacher, no longer wise; he or she has become a little imitation Sauron, a stumbling block and not a bridge.

Tolkien, as a Christian, knew that when God became man to teach us, he asked us to follow him rather than imposing his will on us: gave himself up for us and taught us by example that the greatest love is to lay down our lives for our friends. Gandalf, who gives up his life for his friends on the bridge of Khazad-dûm, is not an allegorical mask for Christ: he is a free creature who freely answers the call to imitate Christ. He and Frodo, who walks his own Way of the Cross, are thus closest to Tolkien's deepest moral ideals.

7. Tolkien's Creation Myth

The collection titled *The Silmarillion* was edited by Christopher Tolkien, J. R. R. Tolkien's son, from the manuscripts left behind by his father. As both Christopher Tolkien and Humphrey Carpenter tell us,[1] there were a number of different versions of each of the works contained in *The Silmarillion,* and one of the reasons that Tolkien himself did not publish the work before his death was his reluctance or inability to choose between different versions. We must, therefore, be cautious of accepting the versions chosen by Christopher Tolkien as representing Tolkien's settled views on some difficult points. But the general trend of the stories casts considerable light on Tolkien's religious imagination.

First, the basically religious character of Tolkien's thought is much clearer in *The Silmarillion* than in the works published earlier. The first book contained in *The Silmarillion* is "Ainulindalë," "The Music of the Ainur." It is basically a creation myth. God, who is referred to as Eru, or more often Ilúvatar, creates first angelic, nonmaterial beings referred to generally as the Ainur, who are with him before anything else was made. Ilúvatar reveals to the Ainur his plan for the creation of the material universe, Arda, and the eventual creation in Arda of the two races of beings with material bodies: first Elves, then human beings. This revelation of Ilúvatar is presented in the form of a Great Music with three major themes.

Except for the mythological presentation of God's revelation as the Great Music, we have here theological ideas familiar to us from the Bible and from Milton's *Paradise Lost:* angels are created before the material universe; God reveals to them something of his plans. But we next have an element original to Tolkien. The themes of creation are laid down by Ilúvatar, but the Ainur are invited to show forth their powers in adorning this theme with their own thoughts and devices. In other words, some elements of the created universe are not directly invented by God but are "variations" of God's creation themes by the angels. (In the next book, the "Valaquenta," we find that the creation of the race of Dwarves is such a "variation" by one of the Ainur.)

It is basic to Christian theology like Tolkien's that only God can truly create, make something out of nothing. In one of his letters, Tolkien says specifically, "The Valar . . . are as we should say angelic powers, whose function is to exercise delegated authority in their spheres (of Rule and government, *not* creation, making or re-making)."[2] This leads to several problems about incidents in the mythology of *The Silmarillion* and in the story of *The Lord of the Rings*. First, how can the Dwarves be creations of one of the Valar if only God can create? Tolkien's most illuminating comment on this is in a draft of a letter in which he is giving the mythological background of *The Lord of the Rings* to an inquirer who had asked some detailed questions about it.

Aulë, for instance, one of the Great, in a sense "fell," for he so desired to see the Children that he became impatient and tried to anticipate the will of the Creator. Being the greatest of all craftsmen he tried to *make* children according to his imperfect knowledge of their kind. When he had made thirteen God spoke to him in anger, but not without pity: for Aulë had done this thing *not* out of evil desire to have slaves and subjects of his own, but out of impatient love, desiring children to talk to and teach, sharing with them the praise of Ilúvatar and his great love of the *materials* of which the world is made. The One rebuked Aulë, saying that he had tried to usurp the Creator's power, but he could not give independent *life* to his makings. He had only one life, his own derived from the One and could at most only distribute it. "Behold," said the One, "these creatures of thine have only thy will, and thy movement. Though you have devised a language for them, they can only report to thee thine own thought. This is a mockery of me."[3]

This passage raised some interesting points not only about Tolkien's conception of creation in the religious sense but about his conception of the kind of "subcreation" done by the author of fiction. The first point is that making or remaking can have good motives, the desire to teach and communicate, or bad motives, the desire to dominate and be worshiped. We will see more of the evil motive when we come to the rebel angels Melkor and Sauron, but this is one of the few cases in which positive motives for creation are discussed by Tolkien.

These positive motives for creation could be applied to God himself. Why does God create human beings? One answer is that he wishes us to know and love him; God creates us to "talk to and teach," to share his delight in his other creations. Aulë, one of the Valar, in his attempt to create persons had motives as close to these as a created being could come: he wished to create "children" to talk to and teach about God and his creation, to share Aulë's own delight in the materials of which the world is made. (The Dwarves, in all of Tolkien's stories, are great craftsmen and appreciate both good material and good making.)

This may seem quite remote and mythological, but it comes home to us very quickly when we ask why we humans desire to have children. To obey and serve us, to "worship" us? That seems to be some people's motives, and we are familiar with the unhappiness that this can cause. If, on the other hand, we have children "to talk to and teach," to share with our own joy in God and God's creation, we are on the right path to a good relationship with them.

Another point raised by this letter is that only God can create genuinely free, autonomous creatures, as he has done in creating human beings. Subcreators, attempting to imitate God as creator, can only "distribute" their own life to their creations. This is true of the author of fiction: we cannot put more into our characters than is in us by inheritance or experience. True enough, our characters may sometimes surprise us, even seem to reveal things to us, but when this happens we are only bringing to light things that were already hidden in our minds or hearts: "they can only report to thee thine own thought."

In the letter cited, Tolkien finishes the story by saying that God forgives Aulë and breathes genuine life into his creations, giving them genuine freedom and full reality. There is a hint in Tolkien's essay "On Fairy Stories" that he thinks that God might someday give independent reality to our fictional creations: "The Christian has still to work, with mind as well as body, to suffer, hope, and die: but he may now perceive that all his bents and faculties have a purpose, which can be redeemed. So great is the bounty with which he has been treated that he may now, perhaps, fairly dare to guess that in Fantasy he may actually assist in the effoliation and multiple enrichment of creation."[4] It may be only a dream for fiction writers that our own creations may someday be given reality by God, but something like this is what Tolkien images for the Valar: their "variations" on God's theme become real.

However, out of this freedom to create variations on Ilúvatar's themes given to the Ainur, Melkor attempts to introduce variations inconsistent with the themes, creating discord. But from this discord Ilúvatar creates greater harmony; in fact, the second and third themes are Ilúvatar's response to Melkor's discords. Here again, familiar theological ideas are given mythological expression: Lucifer, greatest of the angels, is envious of God's power and attempts to make himself a rival of God, but his rebellion is used for good purposes by God's wisdom and power. These ideas, the freedom of the Ainur to make variations on Ilúvatar's themes and Melkor's misuse of this freedom in an effort to spoil Ilúvatar's plans, are an underlying motif of all the books in *The Silmarillion*.

After Ilúvatar has revealed the coming creation of the world to the Ainur, he causes the world he has revealed to come into existence. He sends some of the Ainur into this world to prepare it for Elves and human beings, the "Children of Ilúvatar." The Ainur find the world unshaped, and dark; it is for them to carry out its shaping and lighting according to the vision shown them in the Great Music. Melkor, who covets this new creation as his realm, and its foreshadowed inhabitants as his servants, continually tries to wrest the shaping to his own purposes.

The work of the angelic Ainur as "subcreators" of the world was already a major departure from traditional Judeo-Christian theology: we now get a further departure. The Ainur themselves take on material form, modeled on the form of the to-be-created Elves and Men that they have seen in the Great Music. On entering into the world and taking these forms, they become the Valar, the Powers of the World, and are sometimes referred to as "gods." The Valar are not bound to these material forms but can take them off and put them on as we do clothing, but just as humans are normally clothed, the Valar are normally embodied.

The idea of essentially spiritual beings embodied in this way is an interesting one, and it appears in various legends and stories. A passage in the Old Testament that says that the "sons of God had relations with the daughters of men who bore children to them" (Genesis 6:4) has been interpreted in some para-scriptural legends as meaning that angelic beings took human form and had intercourse with human women. Tolkien mentions one case of this kind, but with the sexes reversed. Melian is one of the Maiar, lesser Ainur who took physical form to help and serve the Valar. She falls in love with and marries Elwë, one of the Elves, and their descendants are some of the wisest and fairest and most powerful of the Elves.

However, except for short and somewhat fragmentary accounts, Tolkien did not do much to exploit the idea of embodied angelic beings and the possibility of their having Elvish or human descendants. When, influenced by Tolkien and Lewis, I wrote some fantasy novels of my own, I took this idea from Tolkien and combined it with Greek mythology.[5] The invented theogony in the background of these stories is that, as in Tolkien, angelic beings are embodied in a human form and are capable of having children with human parents. I identified the original embodied angels with the "Titans," the old gods of Greek mythology, and in my mythology the Olympian gods are partly human, the result of matings between Titan and human. Both the Titans and the Olympians have a mission from God to guide and help human beings, but they are not always faithful to this mission. In place of Tolkien's "Undying Lands" across the Western Sea, I imagined a Bright Land, essentially another dimension, to which only those who are descended from the Titans can go and survive. As in Greek mythology, the Olympians interfere in human affairs, appear to humans, and have human–Olympian children, the demigods of Greek myth.

I mention my own venture into invented myth mainly to contrast it with Tolkien's. After creating a rather elaborate pantheon of "gods," Tolkien in one sense did nothing with it: the Valar play almost no part in the stories in the later part of *The Silmarillion;* much less do they play a part in *The Lord of the Rings.* Occasionally the names of some of the Valar are mentioned, especially that of Varda or Elbereth, one of the Valar who takes a female form and who is spoken of in terms that are reminiscent of traditional Catholic language about the Virgin Mary.

Tolkien's reasons for not making much use of his "gods" are partly artistic, partly theological. Artistically, he wanted the focus of "strangeness" or "magic" to be in the Elves; any kind of anthropomorphic "gods" would have, by contrast, made the Elves seem less magical. Theologically, he was concerned not to show his wise and good characters worshiping false gods of any kind; he solved his problem rather drastically by removing *all* worship from his imagined world. As he says in a letter:

. . . while God (Eru) was a datum of good Númenórean philosophy and a prime fact in their conception of history, He had at the time of the War of the Ring no worship and no hallowed place. And that kind of negative truth was characteristic of the West and all the area under Númenórean influence: the refusal to worship any "creature" and above all no "dark lord" or satanic demon, Sauron, or any other, was almost as far as they got. They had (I imagine) no petitionary prayers to God: but preserved the vestige of thanksgiving. (Those under special Elvish influence might call on the angelic powers for help in immediate peril or fear of evil enemies. The Elves often called on Varda-Elbereth, the Queen of the Blessed Realm; and so does Frodo.)[6]

Artistically, I think that Tolkien's choice was a successful one; his stories have been more widely accepted, more influential for good *because* the religious element is not explicit but is embodied in the story. Theologically, I think his choice is more questionable. Human beings have a need to worship: this appears to be a historical and psychological fact. An atheist will explain this as a human failing that must be resisted; a theist will explain it as one way in which God has "made us for himself," given us tendencies that lead us to him.

To show a human society that has *no* gods, *no* worship, *no* prayers is as untrue to human nature as we know it as it would be to show a society with no love or friendship. Of course worship can be misdirected and can lead to great evils, but so can love or friendship. (C. S. Lewis pointed out that many movements for good *and* for evil in the world have been started by a small group of friends.) In practice, we do not feel the difficulty in *The Lord of the Rings* because of the religious feeling implicit in the story and the fact that Frodo and others *do* call on Elbereth at just the points where a Christian might pray. But when we begin to analyze, we do find a gap in the logic of Tolkien's story. He comes close to implying that a good society (the Shire, Númenor before its fall) can exist without reference to God, and that is not a view that Tolkien really held or would wish to promulgate.

The "Ainulindalë" ends with the embodiment of the Valar and the beginning of conflicts between Melkor and the Valar over the control of Arda, the world; as the Valar form the work, he tries to destroy or distort these forms. Because of Melkor's interference, the Valar are not able to completely carry out either Ilúvatar's original design for the world or their own permitted variations of that design. This is the third major departure from traditional Judeo–Christian theology; the idea that the actual physical form of the universe has been interfered with and spoiled by the Enemy of God, before the Fall of Man.

Tolkien makes it clear that this is the interpretation he intends in a draft of a long letter explaining his mythology to a sympathetic inquirer:

I suppose a difference between this myth and what may be perhaps called Christian mythology is this. In the latter the Fall of Man is subsequent to and a consequent (though not a necessary consequence) of the "Fall of the Angels": a rebellion of created free-will at a higher level than Man; but it is not clearly held (and in many versions is not held at all) that this affected the "World" in its nature: evil was brought in from the outside, by Satan. In this Myth the rebellion of created free-will precedes creation of the world (Eä) and Eä has in it, subcreatively introduced, evil, rebellious, discordant elements in its own nature already when the *Let it Be* was spoken. The fall or corruption, therefore, of all things in it and all inhabitants of it was a possibility if not inevitable. Trees may "go bad" in the Old Forest; Elves may turn to Orcs, and if this required the special pervasive malice of Morgoth, still Elves themselves could do evil deeds. Even the "good" Valar as inhabiting this world could at least err; as the Great Valar did in their dealings with the elves; or as the lesser of their kind (as the Istari or wizards) could in various ways become self-seeking.[7]

Now, of course, what theological status you believe the fall of the angels has depends a good deal on the religious denomination you belong to and whether you are a traditionalist or a "liberal" in theology. As a traditional Catholic, Tolkien would have accepted the traditional Catholic view, but much of this view is theological speculation on the basis of hints in Scripture; very little of it is defined as part of

Catholic doctrine or required to be believed by Catholics as part of their faith. The Fourth Council of the Lateran, for example, declared that "the Devil and the other demons were created good in nature by God, but by their own act they became evil."[8] However, nothing is defined about the time of this occurrence: theological speculation has tended to assume that all the angels fell at the same time, but there is no strong reason to suppose this is correct.

The key point in Tolkien's "myth," however, is that the fall of the angels had an actual physical effect on the world, that some of the harsher and uglier aspects of the material universe may not have been in God's original design. In his book *The Problem of Pain*, which we know was read to the Inklings, C. S. Lewis uses a somewhat similar idea in his discussion of the suffering of animals.

The origin of animal suffering could be traced, by earlier generations, to the Fall of men—the whole world was infected by the uncreating rebellion of Adam. This is now impossible, for we have good reason to believe that animals existed long before men. Carnivorousness, with all that it entails, is older than humanity. Now it is impossible at this point not to remember a certain sacred story which, though never included in the creeds has been widely believed in the Church and seems to be clearly implied in several Dominical, Pauline and Johannine utterances—I mean the story that man was not the first creature to rebel against the Creator, but that some older and mightier being long since became apostate and is now the emperor of darkness and (significantly) the Lord of this world. . . . It seems to me, therefore, a reasonable supposition, that some mighty created power had already been at work for ill in the material universe, or the solar system, or, at least, the planet Earth, before ever man came on the scene: and that when man fell, someone indeed tempted him. This hypothesis is not introduced as a general "explanation of evil": it only gives a wider application of the general principle that evil comes from the abuse of free-will. If there is such a power as I myself believe, it might have corrupted the animal creation before man appeared.[9]

It is hard to say who might have influenced whom in this case: Tolkien's mythology long antedated Lewis's *Problem of Pain* but might not have explicitly contained the idea that the fall of Melkor/Morgoth and his followers in some way spoiled creation. Lewis might have in some sense borrowed from Tolkien, or Tolkien from Lewis, or more likely, they arrived at the general idea independently out of their common Christian tradition. At any rate it is an interesting speculation about the origin of some of the evils in the world.(Of course one must accept the fall of the angels as part of one's belief system for the idea to have any explanatory force.)

A sympathetic critic of Lewis made a point about Lewis's use of this idea that could be applied to Tolkien.

He is driven to favor the speculation of a fall preceding that of Adam: some spiritual prince of this globe fell and corrupted the animals long before man offered him an opportunity for moral seduction. Even so the sum won't add up—if the animals were fallen already, it was as a fallen animal that man acquired the first rudiments of reason.[10]

On one level this criticism is easily disposed of: it confuses a *moral* corruption with a physical "spoiling." Animals are not moral agents, they can be neither innocent nor guilty. So a human inheriting a "corrupted" animal nature does not thereby inherit any *moral* corruption. It might be said that humans might inherit *instincts* or *feelings* that were "spoiled," for instance, an instinct or feeling of aggressiveness. But the traditional doctrine of the Fall says that until humans disobeyed God they were firmly in control of their instincts and emotions; it is only after they rebelled against their Lord that their "unruly members" rebelled against them.

Still, the Lewis suggestion or the Tolkien myth does go against a certain picture we have of the original state of the human race before the Fall as completely innocent and happy: "Eden" and "paradise" carry these associations for us. But perhaps it is our picture at fault, not the Lewis/Tolkien suggestion. Tolkien once said that "a safe Fairyland is false to all worlds."[11] Perhaps a safe paradise, a safe Eden is false to reality too. Perhaps even a safe heaven is also; it may be that in any situation fitted for finite creatures like ourselves, there must be challenge and therefore danger. The speculation would lead us into some rather deep theological waters, but Tolkien's world in which Elves and Men must struggle and strive in a world already made dangerous by Melkor's rebellion has an emotional validity: it seems to have "the taste of primary truth."

The story continues in the "Valaquenta," the "account of the Valar." In it we find that besides the Valar themselves, who are only the greatest of the Ainur Ilúvatar has sent into the world, there are lesser embodied spirits, the Maiar. The Valar themselves are fourteen spirits, seven of whom take male form, seven female form. Like the Greek gods whom, perhaps surprisingly, they resemble rather more than they do the Norse gods, the Valar have divided responsibilities: Manwë rules the sky, Ulmo the sea, and Aulë the earth. Varda, who is called Elbereth by the Elves, is Manwë's consort, and Yavanna, who loves growing things, is the consort of Aulë. Of the major Vala (singular of *Valar*), Ulmo has no consort, nor does Nienna, a female Vala who seems to be especially associated with compassion and healing. Again, the notion of angelic beings as male and female and as paired off in something like marriage is a departure from Judeo-Christian angelology, although there are some hints of it in the byways of Judaic theology.

Of Melkor we are told that he is the only Vala to turn away from Ilúvatar, but he corrupts many of the Maiar, some before his evil is apparent but some at a later time—as we saw, a departure from traditional angelology, in which all of the fallen angels turn against God at the same time. (The Balrogs are identified as fallen Maiar, which fits in with hints given in the trilogy.)

Before going on the "Silmarillion" proper, which is called the "Quenta Silmarillion," or "History of the Silmarils," let us ask ourselves whether the creation myth of the "Ainulindalë" and the transmutation of the angels into something like pagan gods alters our picture of Tolkien as basically a Christian writer. To answer this question we must ask ourselves what Tolkien was trying to do in these stories. They are certainly not attempts to rewrite the Genesis account or even to interpret it; that is, Tolkien does not propose them as subjects for primary belief either for himself or for us. What they are is an attempt to create myth as a kind of literature, commanding secondary, not primary, belief. The Christian artists of the Renaissance used pagan mythology in their painting and sculpture not because they believed in pagan mythology but because it offered them artistically interesting themes. Tolkien, who enjoyed myth as a literary experience, was moved to try his own hand at myth making.

When we look at *The Silmarillion* as a whole, we find that it fits perfectly the description of myth given by C. S. Lewis. The stories of *The Silmarillion* "depend hardly at all on such usual narrative attractions as suspense or surprise. . . . Human sympathy is at a minimum. . . . The experience may be sad or joyful but it is always grave . . . not only grave but awe-inspiring." And as Lewis says of myth in general, there is a numinous element in *The Silmarillion;* "It is as if something of great moment had been communicated to us."[12]

A private mythology may seem an eccentric kind of literary creation, but I can see no reason to rule it out as illegitimate. There seems no reason why those who enjoy myth as Tolkien did cannot create their own myths for enjoyment. That this was Tolkien's own view of what he was doing we have evidence in some of his letters quoted earlier.

When we arrive at the "Quenta Silmarillion," we again begin with an account of "the beginning of days," a myth not of the creation but of the mythical prehistory of the world. These first several chapters play somewhat the same role that an account of Theseus might play in the history of Athens or the story of Romulus and Remus in a history of Rome; they are feigned myth, whereas the rest of the "Quenta Silmarillion" is feigned history with mythological elements. The material given in these early chapters confirms several guesses that could be made on the basis of information in the trilogy. It is true that Elves do not truly die: Tolkien tells us that when an Elf is killed his spirit goes to the "Halls of Mandos" and the Elf may eventually return to Arda in embodied form (though no instance of this is given). That the "Uttermost West" is the home of the Valar, that Eressëa is an island to the east of it where Elves lived, and that Númenor was on an island somewhat to the east of Eressëa is all hinted at in *The Lord of the Rings* but developed in *The Silmarillion:* a number of the Elves live on Valinor, the island in the Uttermost West, and Eressëa is a smaller island in a bay on the east side of Valinor where only some of the Elves live.

In the "Quenta Silmarillion" the world was flat before the action of Eru in removing Valinor and Eressëa from "the circles of the world." Tolkien does not hesitate to be unashamedly mythological and unscientific in his account; in his story the stars are created long after the creation of Earth, and the sun and moon are created last of all. For some time the world has no lights in the sky and then for a while the light of the stars, which are created by Varda. The light of the lands of the world before the raising of the sun and moon is provided at first by two "lamps" set on high pillars; when Melkor destroys these, the Valar light the Land of Aman, which is Valinor, the Uttermost West, with two radiant trees, leaving the rest of the world in twilight under the light of the stars created by Varda. Eventually Melkor destroys these Trees too, but before this several key events have occurred. The Elves have been created and awake in "Middle-earth," the central part of the flat world imagined by Tolkien. Later on they are called by the Valar to the West to live in the light of the Two Trees under the protection of the Valar. Part of the Elves, the Vanyar and the Noldor, come all the way to Valinor, some, the Teleri, come later and more reluctantly. Not all of them come all the way, and those that do at first land on Eressëa rather than on Valinor. Some Elves, the Avari, refuse to leave Middle-earth at all. The reluctance of some Elves and the refusal of others is due to lies and rumors spread by Melkor, who continually acts to spoil the plans of the Valar and turn Elves and humans away from Ilúvatar. Even after the Vanyar and the Noldor are established in Valinor and the Teleri begin to come from Eressëa to Valinor, Melkor continues his subtle plots. One of the greatest of the Noldor, Fëanor, creates three marvelous jewels, the Silmarils, which have some of the light of the Two Trees in them. After subtly poisoning the attitude of the Noldor to the Valar, Melkor strikes physically, killing the Two Trees, and steals the Silmarils. Influenced by his love of his creations and the lies of Melkor, Fëanor leads a great many of the Noldor back to Middle-earth, swearing vengeance on Melkor and seeking independence from the Valar. To get the ships of the Teleri, who have become great seafarers, Fëanor leads the first war of Elf against Elf; the vanguard of his group become killers of their own race, and even those who do not take part in the attack become guilty of complicity by continuing with Fëanor (some of the group repent and turn back).

This and subsequent incidents force us to give up the idea we might get from *The Lord of the Rings* that the Elves are a wholly good race. Under the influence of Melkor they can kill, covet, and steal, but as opposed to human beings, who are a fallen race, it is individual Elves, always under some influence from Melkor, who sin, and their sin does not affect other Elves except as those Elves voluntarily make themselves part of the sin. In Adam all men fell, but by Fëanor only some Elves are led astray.

As the story of the Silmarils unfolds, the battle between good and evil moves to a more physical level. Melkor attacks with Balrogs, dragons, and hordes of Orcs the "immigrant" Elves and those who have stayed in Middle-earth. We learn that Orcs are the descendants of corrupted Elves, explaining the horror with which they are regarded by Elves and confirming that evil powers can only corrupt, not create. After causing all sorts of trouble and sorrow, two of the Silmarils are destroyed; the other is returned to the Valar and becomes the Evening Star. These later parts of the "Quenta Silmarillion" are more "realistic"; there are battles, chases, the building of strongholds and their betrayal, stories of happy and unhappy love. But underlying everything is the unending battle between good and evil; Melkor is eventually captured and exiled into the Outer Dark, but his lieutenant, Sauron, takes up the battle on the side of evil.

The remaining books of *The Silmarillion* are the "Akallabêth"—Tolkien's version of the Atlantis legend—and a brief account, "Of the Rings of Power and the Third Age." These books expand material already in the appendices of *The Lord of the Rings* and contain few surprises for those who have studied those appendices. Like *The Lord of the Rings, The Silmarillion* ends with geneologies and indexes of names and contains fascinating and evocative maps.

In general, *The Silmarillion* deepens but does not change our assessment of J. R. R. Tolkien. As might be expected, the work as a whole is so logical and well knit that many guesses made on the basis of hints in the earlier work can be confirmed. Much is revealed, but much is held back. We can guess that the *Istari,* the Wizards, are Maiar, but this is not clearly stated in *The Silmarillion:* we have to confirm this from Tolkien's letters. The "Secret Fire" or "Hidden Fire" mentioned in some important contexts is unexplained; Tolkien told an inquirer that the term refers to the Holy Spirit.[13] Tolkien keeps some of his reticences.

In particular, there is no hint or mention, despite their deep importance to Tolkien, of Christ or Christianity. If *The Silmarillion* seems to end on a somewhat dark and despairing note, it is because Tolkien has not allowed himself to introduce any hint of the true Hope of the World. Partly, this is his personal reticence; partly it is his artistic purpose. But the Christian hope is in Tolkien's own heart and is hidden in the heart of his work.

8. Magic and Miracle in Middle-earth

Tolkien's use of magic in his stories is quite sparing. In *The Hobbit* it is confined to Bilbo's use of the magic ring to make himself invisible and a few uses of magical fire by Gandalf. In *The Lord of the Rings* there are more uses of the Ring for invisibility and more fire-magic by Gandalf. There are several cases of clairvoyance and possibly of mind reading. Those involving Galadriel have already been mentioned: there are also cases involving use of the Palantíri, "crystal balls" that enable their user to see events at a distance and perhaps see into the minds of others. The Ring, it is revealed, gives a sort of immortality to its wearer, and exhibits a sort of semi-animate quasi-purposiveness, seeming to "tempt" Frodo to use it in circumstances that might reveal its presence or give away its location to its original maker.

One of Tolkien's few discussions of magic in a general way is in a draft of a letter. He begins by making a distinction between *magia,* which achieves actual effects in the world, and *goeteia,* which merely creates illusions.

Neither is, in this tale good or bad (per se) but only by motive, purpose or use. Both sides use both, but with different motives. The supremely bad motive is (for this tale, since it is especially about it) domination of other "free" wills. The Enemy's operations are by no means all goetic deceits, but "magic" that produces real effects in the physical world. But his *magia* he uses to bulldoze both people and things and his *goeteia* to terrify and subjugate. Their *magia* Gandalf and the elves use (sparingly): a *magia* producing real results (like fire in a wet faggot) for specific benevolent purposes. Their goetic effects are entirely *artistic* and are not intended to deceive: they never deceive Elves (but may deceive or bewilder unaware Men) since the difference to them is as clear as the difference to us between painting, sculpture, and "life."

Both sides live mainly by ordinary means. . . . The basic motive for *magia*

—quite apart from any philosophical questions of how it would work—is immediacy: speed, reduction of labor, and reduction to a minimum (or vanishing point) of the gap between the idea or desire and the result or effect. But the magia may not be easy to come by and at any rate if you have command of abundant slave labor or machinery (often only the same thing concealed) it may be as quick or quick enough to push mountains over, wreck forests or build pyramids by such means. . . .

Anyway a difference in the use of "magic" in this story is that it is not to be come by by lore or spells: but is an inherent power not possessed or attainable by Men as such.[1]

There are several interesting points here. The distinction between *magia* and *goeteia* to a large extent parallels the twofold nature of the Elves as "scientists" and "artists" or, rather, as idealizations of the scientific and artistic elements in human beings.

We see that whereas the Enemy uses *goeteia* to "deceive and terrify," the Elves use it only as a form of art and are always clearly aware of the difference between art and reality. There is an implied moral here as to the proper use of art that recalls some things in "Leaf by Niggle": Councillor Tompkins wants to use art only as propaganda, whereas the whole tenor of the story is that art should be "appreciative," should express a vision of or reaction to the world.

The use of *magia* or technology (including machinery) to control the *world* is not itself evil. Tolkien says: it depends on the motive. However, the use of magic or technology to control free wills is always evil: it is clear enough what Tolkien would say about brainwashing or other forms of mind control by technological means. However, even the use of machinery or technology to control the material world is dangerous: it makes our action on the world more rapid and more powerful, thus enormously "amplifying" mistaken or malicious choices. Long before the effects of environmental pollution began to cause general alarm, Tolkien was an instinctively "ecological" thinker.

As Tolkien said in a letter to his son Christopher:

There is the tragedy and despair of all machinery laid bare. Unlike art which is content to create a new secondary world in the mind, it attempts to actualize desire and so to create power in this World; and that cannot be done with any real satisfaction. Laboursaving machinery only creates endless and worse labour. And in addition to this fundamental disability of a creature, is added the Fall, which makes our devices not only fail at their desire but turn to new and horrible evil. So we come inevitably from Daedalus and Icarus to the Giant Bomber. It is not an advance in wisdom![2]

When he first wrote these words, Tolkien might have been regarded by most people as merely "reactionary," opposed to the "blessings" of science and progress. Now more and more people are beginning to criticize the ideal of continuous progress and the increased technologization of life. The ideal of *limited* use of technology *(magia)* "for *specific* benevolent purposes" and a keen awareness that television, films, and so on are *not* real life seems more and more to be a reasonable ideal.

In some ways, therefore, magic in Tolkien's stories is being used as a metaphor for art and for technology. But it is also an underlying feature of Tolkien's Middle-earth: his secondary world is a world where "magic works." For some critics this *ipso facto* means that Tolkien's stories cannot be real literature, cannot be taken seriously. This is true even of some critics who take science fiction seriously; because science fiction is based on extrapolated science, it is for them "realistic" in a way in which fantasy is not. There are some critics who see the current popularity of fantasy as a threat to the "scientific outlook" fostered by science fiction and as a manifestation of an "escapist," "unrealistic" view of life. What is the basis of this hostility to magic and fantasy?

There is a view of the world that to many people seems obviously true, the merest common sense. According to this view, our minds can affect other minds or the world around us only through the medium of our bodies. If I want you to understand me, I cause my body to make vibrations in the air or marks on paper, which affect your ears or eyes and through them your mind. If I want to affect nearby matter on a small scale, moving a chair for example, I use my body directly. If I want to affect matter at a distance or on a large scale, I use my body to set up chains of physical causation, for example, to fire a missile or operate a bulldozer. Thus, on this view, our minds are "insulated" from other minds and from matter apart from our body; for convenience, I will call this view the insulated view of mind and matter.

This view does not in itself presuppose any view about what minds are. I have used ordinary language to describe the view and, rightly or wrongly, ordinary language is dualistic; it assumes that our minds are different from our bodies. But if you identify the mind and the brain you can restate the view in terms of brain and body. On the other hand, if you hold that the mind is a nonmaterial substance, you could restate the view in terms of soul and body. Dualists as well as materialists can hold the insulated view; materialists as well as dualists can deny it. Whether the insulated view is true is a separate question from whether dualism or materialism is true.

There are a number of views incompatible with the insulated view, but there are two historically important views that are incompatible with it in rather different ways. The first of these is what I will call the primitive view; many people at many times have held such a view, and probably all of us at some time have been tempted to accept it. According to this view, our thoughts, desires, and wishes can sometimes affect other minds or the material universe directly, without the intervention of our bodies, and furthermore, we can sometimes affect other minds or the material universe by symbolic means, using our bodies to speak words or perform actions that do not set up chains of physical causation, at least in any ordinary sense. For example, the witch doctor sticks pins into the image of his enemy, hoping to give that enemy pains in the corresponding portions of his anatomy, or the witch recites incantations hoping to blight her enemies' crops.

The rejection of the primitive view is often equated with "mental maturity" or "a realist attitude." Here are two quotations to that effect, one from Thornton Wilder's "historical fantasy" *The Ides of March,* the second from a book column by Algis Budrys in *The Magazine of Fantasy and Science Fiction.* In Wilder's book, Julius Caesar writes to a longtime friend:

"From you I learned, but slowly, that there are large fields of experience which our longing cannot alter and which our fears cannot forfend. I clung for years to a host of self-delusions, to the belief that burning intensity in the mind can bring a message from an indifferent loved one and that sheer indignation can halt the triumphs of an enemy. The universe goes its mighty way and there is very little we can do to modify it. You remember how shocked I was when you let fall so light the words 'Hope has never changed tomorrow's weather.' "[3]

In the book column, Budrys is discussing the worldview characteristic of what he calls "modern" science fiction:

The fundamental discovery that the Universe does not care; it simply works. There is no way to repeal or amend physical laws. The rich, the poor, the holy and the unholy are all subject to hunger, thirst, pain and death. Civilization of whatever kind, is a response to the discovery that community action at least offers hope of relief to all. Most human history represents the ongoing attempt to work out a plan whereby that relief is in fact distributed to all rather than merely to some. Technological action—exploring physical possibilities and applying deft means of conveying maximum comfort to the maximum number of individuals offers the best hope, magic showing a very poor record in that respect. (And yet how appealing it is to think that simply displaying the proper attitude might modify the Universe! It's a hope we somehow cannot bring ourselves to abandon. Hence John W. Campbell's interest in fantasy. He was a humanist.)[4]

I am not calling the primitive view "primitive" in a necessarily unfavorable sense; as Budrys's last words suggest, it may be "primitive" in the sense of "basic" or "ineradicable." But we need to consider one further view, which has also been held by many people at many times and is still held by many people today: I will call it the animistic view. According to this view, there exist nonmaterial minds or spirits that can affect matter and embodied minds directly. Our minds can affect other embodied minds and affect the material universe through the intermediary of these nonmaterial minds or spirits, and we affect the nonmaterial minds or spirits, either by thinking or by speech or other symbolic actions.

Notice that the animistic view, as I have defined it, covers at one extreme the traditional Christian theist, praying either mentally or verbally or by some ceremony such as the Catholic Mass to a nonmaterial person, God, for good weather or peace in the Middle East or consolation for a suffering friend. At the other extreme, the animistic view takes in the medieval or Renaissance magician invoking devils with spells and pentagrams to raise a storm, cause a war, or afflict an enemy. Both cases presuppose an animistic view (in my technical sense of "animistic," not necessarily in a dictionary sense).

In many books intended to introduce science fiction and/or fantasy to those not familiar with the field, you will notice a curious shilly-shallying about the difference between science fiction and fantasy. Typically, the author starts off by stating confidently that the difference consists of the fact that science fiction deals with what is scientifically possible, fantasy with what is not scientifically possible. Then the author loses his or her nerve a bit, because after all faster-than-light travel is, so far as we know, scientifically impossible, and much modern science fiction could not do without it; the solar system is now too small for science fiction. And then there is that good old science fiction theme, time travel, which may be not only scientifically, but somehow logically, impossible. So the grand generalization dies away in a flurry of qualifications, and the author tactfully changes the subject.

Broadly speaking and subject to qualifications, science fiction is happiest with the insulated view, can tolerate some versions of the primitive view, and is extremely uneasy with any version of the animistic view, whereas almost all fantasy presupposes either the animistic view or a version of the primitive view rather different from that popular in science fiction.

In Tolkien we have pure fantasy. In fantasy, "magic works" (that is practically a definition of fantasy). And the magic is that of the primitive view, worked directly and not by means of spirits. Gandalf mutters a spell, and a fire lights at the end of his staff, or a locked door opens. Galadriel lends clairvoyance to Sam and Frodo, and it is hinted that she can read thoughts. Nobody ever tries to explain how such things work, they simply do. In C. S. Lewis we have a fully animistic view: the Eldila of the space trilogy (or Ransom trilogy) are disembodied spirits with some characteristics of angels and some of Neoplatonic Intelligences. Furthermore, God himself, under the pseudonym of Maleldil, plays an important role in the story.

It has been said that all human conflicts are basically theological. That is as true as most generalizations and truer than many. A good many attempts to draw the line between science fiction and fantasy are in fact "theological": those who share the "scientific," materialistic view that dominates the intellectual culture of Western nations attempt to hold the realm of science fiction for that view and to read out of the canon as heretical stories based on animistic views or primitive views that do not pay suitable obeisance to science.

If, on the other hand, we use the distinction between stories that assume the insulated view and those that do not merely as a classificatory device with no value implications, it can help solve an important problem. The problem is this: it is notoriously difficult to give any adequate definition of "science fiction," and this clouds efforts to theorize about the field.

As we saw in Chapter 3, one can delineate the field of science fiction by listing its characteristic themes. Science fiction often deals with the future, with space travel, with off-Earth locations, with time travel, with telepathy or other "psi" powers, with alien beings, or with discoveries or machines that are beyond the present scope of science. A "cluster definition" of science fiction can be given by saying that a story is science fiction if one or more of these themes is present to an important degree. Fantasy, as we said, can be given a similar cluster definition. It tends to deal with the distant and legendary past or with pastlike "alternative worlds," with magical means of travel or communication, with "other worlds"—usually Earth-like—reached by magical means, with magical powers and objects, and with nonhuman beings that resemble those in folklore or mythology.

However, when we try to give a *general* definition that states a factor common to science fiction but not to fantasy or to fantasy but not to science fiction, we run into difficulties. To distinguish *both* of those sorts of stories from "mundane" literature is not impossible: we can talk of "secondary worlds" as Tolkien did, or of "alternative worlds." The point is that the worlds of science fiction and fantasy are *structurally* different from the real world, different not just in the addition of invented characters or incidents but in some major way.

I think that this idea can be made sufficiently precise to serve as a delimitation of speculative fiction from mundane fiction, though there are many difficulties involved. But, to date, a further delimitation of science fiction and fantasy has suffered from the difficulty that I pointed out earlier: you cannot demarcate the "alternative worlds" of science fiction from those of fantasy in terms of "scientific possibility," since so many of the standard themes of science fiction (notably faster-than-light travel) would fall on the wrong side of the line.

To this dilemma I think the distinctions I have made may provide an answer. An "alternative world" story is science fiction if it assumes the insulated view, fantasy if it assumes the primitive or animistic views. I think that this suggestion will give us intuitively satisfactory classification in most cases and at least a reasonable classification in borderline cases. For example, the work of C. S. Lewis is fantasy on the suggested classification, despite the spaceships in the Ransom trilogy, because it assumes an animistic view. On the other hand, some stories marketed as fantasy are science fiction, despite the use of some potent fantasy symbols and echoes of some fantasy themes, because basically they assume an insulated view.

No doubt my suggestion will lead to some counterintuitive classifications, though I cannot come up with any at this time. But it has one great virtue: since the other two views in question are incompatible with the insulated view, no story can assume *both* the insulated view and one or both of the others. Thus, on the suggested classification scheme no story can be both science fiction and fantasy.

Nothing will prevent some people from using the scheme I recommend as an evaluative device, arguing that, since the insulated view is true and the other views are false, this makes science fiction (as it is defined here) superior to fantasy. So long as they mean by "superior" only "nearer to the actual state of affairs" and not "superior as literature" or "more valuable to the reader," then if we grant that the insulated view is true, we can hardly deny that science fiction is closer to the truth than fantasy is. This criterion is a two-edged sword, of course: if our major concern is staying close to the way things actually are, we will reject all speculative literature in favor of the mundane, realistic story.

But not everyone will agree that the insulated view is in fact the truth, or at least the whole truth. The question is, in the end, a philosophical rather than scientific one, involving as it does views about the nature of reality based on an interpretation of our total experience.

So if someone says, "I enjoy science fiction more than fantasy because I agree with the insulated view and feel uncomfortable with stories based on the primitive or animistic views," that reader is at least being more honest than a good many critics of fantasy. I think, though, that such a person might profit from reading stories based on assumptions he or she disagrees with, if only to understand better the view that is being rejected.

How is magic related to religion? As I have defined the animistic view, it is so broad as to include action by God in response to prayer. Therefore, a traditional theist who believes that God sometimes answers prayers would *ipso facto* be accepting an animistic view in my sense, and insofar as the insulated view is incompatible with the animistic view, it is incompatible with traditional theism. On the other hand, there is an important distinction between magic as a sort of technology, which always works when the proper procedures are followed, and prayer that is a request to a person, a request that may be refused. A traditional theist may be entirely skeptical about animistic magic in the usual sense, holding that humans have no powers to *compel* spirits.

In fact, traditional theists with a clear, developed theology about what spiritual beings exist and the limits of their powers may have specific theological reasons for rejecting certain accounts of magic. For example, they may hold that human beings are essentially *embodied* spirits, that our souls can only act on our bodies and on no other matter. This would eliminate the primitive view. Furthermore, in most traditional theologies, Jewish and Christian, that accept the existence of spiritual beings less than God, these spiritual beings are superior to humans and could not be controlled or compelled by humans. An angel might be commanded by God to affect matter in some way in response to human prayers. A demon might use its powers as a spirit to achieve certain effects, in an effort to tempt or deceive human beings. But magic as a "technology" for achieving material effects by the co-operation of spiritual beings would be *theologically* impossible. (In fact, a position rather like this has been held by Catholic theologians.)

In Tolkien's secondary world of Middle-earth, "magic works." Since Gandalf and Saruman are in fact angelic beings temporarily embodied in humanlike form, it would be quite compatible with this theological view if they were able to affect matter directly by the use of their wills, for on many traditional theological views angels would have such a power.

It is more puzzling why the Elves would have such a power if, like humans, they are embodied spirits. However, the Elves are not embodied spirits in quite the same way humans are: they are immortal so long as the physical universe lasts, and if they are killed in Middle-earth their spirits go to the Halls of Mandos and eventually return to Middle-earth re-embodied. Thus the relation of body and spirit in Elves is in some ways more like the relation of the Valar and the Maiar to their temporary embodiments than it is like the human body-soul relation. Thus it is less surprising that Elves might have extra powers of affecting matter directly by an action of their mind or spirit.

That there *could* exist beings like Tolkien's Elves seems compatible with Catholic theology, and Tolkien was concerned to keep within those limits as much as he could. As he says in one letter:

The cycles begin with a cosmogonical myth: the Music of the Ainur. God and the Valar (or powers: Englished as gods) are revealed. The latter are as we should say angelic powers. . . . On the side of mere narrative device this is, of course, meant to provide beings of the same order, power and majesty as the "gods" of higher mythology, which can be yet accepted—well, shall we say baldly, by a mind that believes in the Blessed Trinity.[5]

Tolkien also defended his views against an intelligent and sympathetic Catholic critic who questioned some of the philosophical and theological ideas in *The Lord of the Rings,* including the idea of the sort of "reincarnation" that occurs when an Elf is killed in Middle-earth.

We differ entirely about the nature of the relation of sub-creation to Creation. I should have thought that liberation "from the channels the creator is known to have used already" is a fundamental function of sub-creation, a tribute to the infinity of His potential variety, one of the ways in which indeed it is exhibited, as indeed I said in the Essay. I am not a metaphysician; but I should have thought it a curious metaphysic—there is not one but many, indeed potentially innumerable ones—that declared the channels known (in such a finite corner as we have any inkling of) to have been used, are the only possible ones or efficacious, or possibly acceptable to and by Him!

Reincarnation may be bad *theology* (that surely rather than metaphysics) as applied to Humanity, and my *legendarium,* especially the Downfall of Nú-menor which lies immediately behind *The Lord of the Rings* is based on my view: that Men are essentially mortal and must not seek to become immortal in the flesh. But I do not see how even in the Primary World any theologian or philosopher, unless very much better informed about the relation of spirit and body than I believe anyone to be, could deny the *possibility* of re-incarnation as a mode of existence prescribed for certain kinds of rational incarnate creatures.[6]

Here we see Tolkien taking the position that there may be a number of different *philosophical* views compatible with religious truth as re-vealed by God. Some Catholics have been inclined to challenge this and hold that there is only one philosophical view, Thomism perhaps, that is "really Catholic." From evidence in Tolkien's reply to the letter, his critic seems somewhat inclined to take this position. Tolkien, though on some matters conservative and even somewhat "reactionary," took a more "liberal" view on this issue as well as some other religious issues, such as ecumenism. ·

As a writer of fiction, a creator of legend, Tolkien claimed a "sub-creator's" freedom to explore possible variations on the themes of the original creation—the same freedom he gave the Ainur in his creation myth. So far as his beliefs about the primary world were concerned, Tolkien was a traditional, orthodox Catholic. So far as his subcreated world was concerned, he claimed the right to say, not how things are, but how, within the limits set by his fundamental beliefs, they *could* be.

As a traditional Catholic, Tolkien accepted the existence of miracles. In his stories there is only one event that might be called miraculous in the strict sense, and it is not part of the "told" story but only part of the background mythology recounted in the appendices to *The Lord of the Rings* and in *The Silmarillion.* Here is the brief and cryptic account in appendix I of *The Lord of the Rings:*

There was rebellion and strife in Númenor . . . Ar-Pharazôn the Golden was the proudest and most powerful of all the Kings, and no less than the kingdom of the world was his desire. . . . He prepared the greatest armament that the world had seen, and when all was ready set sail: and he broke the Ban of the

Valar, going up with war to wrest everlasting life from the Lords of the West. But when Ar-Pharazôn set foot on the shores of Aman the Blessed, the Valar lay down their Guardianship and called upon the One and the world was changed. Númenor was thrown down and swallowed in the Sea and the Undying Lands were removed for ever from the circles of the world.[7]

The account in the "Akallabêth," the extended account of the history of Númenor, is hardly more detailed with regard to the miraculous event.

At last Ar-Pharazôn came even to Aman, the Blessed Realm, and the coasts of Valinor: and still all was silent and doom hung by a thread. For Ar-Pharazôn wavered at the end and almost he turned back. His heart misgave him when he looked upon the soundless shores and saw Taniquetil shining, whiter than snow, colder than death, silent, immutable, terrible as the shadow of Ilúvatar. But pride was now his master, and at last he left his ship and strode upon the shores, claiming the land for his own. . . .

Then Manwë upon the mountain called upon Ilúvatar and for that time the Valar laid down their government of Arda. But Ilúvatar showed forth his power and he changed the fashion of the world and a great chasm opened in the sea between Númenor and the Deathless Lands and the waters flowed down into it, and the noise and the smoke of the cataracts went up to heaven and the world was shaken. . . .

But the land of Aman and Eressëa of the Eldar were taken away and removed beyond the reach of men forever. . . . And . . . Númenor . . . was utterly destroyed. . . . For Ilúvatar cast back the Great Seas . . . and new lands and seas were made; and the world was diminished, for Valinor and Eressëa were taken from it into the realm of hidden things.[8]

This event was a miracle in the strongest sense: it was a direct intervention of God into the world in such a way that normal physical laws and processes were suspended. There is a good dramatic description of events leading up to and following the miracle, but nowhere in any published material does Tolkien say much more about the miracle itself.

There are good literary reasons for this, because it is difficult if not impossible to write a convincing story in which miracle plays too large a part. By definition miracles are an intervention from outside of ordinary life that cannot be expected, counted on, or prepared for.

Unless you take on the impossible task of writing a story from God's point of view, there is no way in which you can show a miracle as an event following from the characters and circumstances of the story, and it is very hard to make an incident convincing if it does not follow from what has gone before in a story in a way that *seems,* at least, natural. (We are more aware of, and more suspicious of, mere chance or coincidence in stories than in real life.)

Gandalf's return from apparent death after his battle with the Balrog on the Bridge of Khazad-dûm is not, I believe, intended to be a miracle: there seems no reason to believe that God has intervened directly, and it seems within the "natural" abilities of embodied Ainur to re-form their bodily "clothing" after it has been damaged or even destroyed. But just because it is not a miracle, Tolkien can prepare us for it by hints about the powers and mission of Gandalf. He is sent by the Valar to be the opponent of Sauron; until Sauron is defeated his mission is not over. When Sauron is defeated, Gandalf eventually returns to the Blessed Realm, his work done, his mission accomplished.

For some authors it would be overtheoretical to discuss at such length the reason for the use of magic and even a miracle in a story; their only purpose is to tell an exciting story, and people have always found the marvelous exciting. But although Tolkien is very much concerned to tell a good tale, his underlying purposes are most serious: he wishes to express a view of life with room for freedom and immortality, for the natural and the supernatural, a view of life that can be accepted "by a mind that believes in the Blessed Trinity."

9. Frodo, Fëanor, and Free Will

As Tolkien remarks in passing in a letter quoted in the last chapter, "the supremely bad motive is (for this tale, since it is especially about it) domination of other 'free wills.' "[1] The evils of dominating other wills and the value of freedom are an important theme in both *The Lord of the Rings* and *The Silmarillion*. Frodo and Fëanor may be taken as symbolizing the right use of free will and the wrong use. Frodo accepts his mission as Ring-bearer, and though he endures much suffering, he gains tremendous spiritual growth and is able to bring "salvation" to those he loves. Fëanor, the great Elvish craftsman, refuses to accept his destiny and as a result diminishes in stature, becoming a tool of Melkor, and causes his kindred and followers to be exiled from the Blessed Land.

Thus Fëanor acts out to some extent the role of Adam, who brought evil into the world by disobedience, whereas Frodo in a limited way acts out the role of Christ, defeating evil by obedience and self-sacrifice. Underlying these two stories is a Christian view of what free will is and how it should be used. On this view, persons (humans, Hobbits, Elves, Dwarves, Ents) are genuinely free: able to disobey Ilúvatar and the Valar. However, disobedience always has its cost: unhappiness for the one who disobeys and for others. Choices are not irrevocable: Gollum and Saruman and Denethor are offered chances to repent and refuse, whereas Galadriel, Boromir, and Théoden all at some point repent and change.

Tolkien often gives us pairs of characters faced with basically the same problem and shows one handling the problem in the right way, the other in the wrong way: Théoden and Denethor, the king who changes and the king who refuses to change; Frodo, who succeeds as Ring-bearer, Gollum, who is destroyed by the Ring. Sometimes the contrasts are more complex, as in the cases of Gandalf and Saruman, Boromir and Faramir, who are contrasted in a number of ways. Insofar as it can be said that characters from two different stories (though with the same underlying mythology) are contrasted, I think that Galadriel is the intended contrast character to Fëanor; her rejection of the Ring contrasts with his refusal to give up the Silmarils.

The fact that one character fails and the other does not, in what is essentially the same situation, is one way of dramatizing in fiction the idea of genuine free will, the idea that a person can make choices that are not determined by his or her character or circumstances. We can show this dramatically either by showing one person making a wrong choice then a right choice (or vice versa) in basically the same circumstances or else by showing two people in the same circumstances, one of whom makes the right choice the other the wrong choice.

Those who challenge the idea of free will usually do so in one of two ways. They may try to show that all of our actions are in fact determined in some way, or they may challenge the notion of choice involved in the free will view by arguing that such choices would be arbitrary because uncaused. In fiction, especially fantasy fiction, a way of expressing the idea that all our actions are determined is to show everything as determined by Fate or Destiny. A way of challenging the idea of free choice is to show choices being made in such a way that we feel that no other choice *could* have been made in those circumstances.

On the other hand, someone who wants to express a free will view in fiction will show us characters who are *not* constrained by Fate or Destiny or show us situations in which we feel that either of two choices *could* have been made by the character involved. An author may attempt, however, to show the *interplay* of fate and free will, as Tolkien does. Bilbo was *meant* to find the Ring, but whether he is strong enough to pass it on to Frodo is genuinely in doubt. It is Frodo's destiny to be the Ring-bearer, but he may shirk that destiny, either by refusing it at the beginning or by failing to carry out his mission.

Someone who approaches a "free will" story with determinist presuppositions can read it against the author's intentions. Some writers about Tolkien have said that Gollum "couldn't help" betraying Frodo, that his previous experiences *plus* Sam's harsh words at a crucial moment *determine* his later actions. Other critics have emphasized the role of destiny in Tolkien and ignored the role of choice, implying that the issues are never in doubt that the heroes *must* be heroic, the villains *must* be villainous. Here, for example, is a rather biased piece of criticism by a generally insightful critic and writer of science fiction, Joanna Russ:

"Heroic fantasy" (is) that form of twentieth century escapism pillaged from genuine medieval culture. . . . Rocky caverns full of rank stench inhabited by evil entities with red eyes, sentences like "Peace lay over the realm of the Wide Land," and other signs of Secondary Universes in the brewage only send me into fits of giggling followed by stupefying boredom. . . . George Bernard Shaw once said that those who have grappled face to face with reality have little patience with fools' paradises, and another political radical, Virginia Woolf, stated flatly that "books of sensation and adventure" quickly grow dull because they can only present the same kind of thrill over and over. Susie Charnas once wrote to me about the fixity of Lewis' and Tolkien's characters: "Arrowshirt, son of Arrowroot, son of Stuffed Shirt, THIS IS YOUR VIRTUE!" In short, fiction's only real subject is the changes that occur in human beings, and since real change is the one thing that "heroic fantasy" (with its aim of wish-fulfillment) must avoid at all costs, such fantasies often begin with a delicious sense of freedom and possibility, only to turn dismayingly familiar and stale unless well salted with comedy or adorned with rapidly changing, interesting, and colorful scenery. C. S. Lewis, who is very good at scenery, manages in this way partly to disguise the dreadful predictability of his Narnia books—i.e., aristocrats stay noble, dwarves cunning, animals loyal, and peasants stupid unless pushed by God or the Devil. After the marvelous opening of *The Lion, the Witch, and the Wardrobe,* Lewis can find no story for his world but Christian myth imposed like a straitjacket over the plot and no antagonist but that old sexist stereotype, the proud, independent, and therefore wicked, woman. Nor does George MacDonald fare any better. What to do in these wonderful Other worlds is always the problem, for although reality can't be escaped (it being all there is), it can be impoverished and sooner or later the mechanical predictability of the whole awful business sends you back to such comparatively heartening works as "The Penal Colony" or "The Death of Ivan Ilyitch" where there is humanity, contingency, and reality.

The desire for escape is understandable. It's the supply that's spurious. Unfortunately, after Tolkien had wrung the last drop of meaning-freighted landscape out of an extremely tiny genre, the cry went up, "Now we know how to do it!" and another, "There's money in it!" and the flood began.

With orthodox heroic fantasy, one judges the quality not of books but of guided daydreams . . . such novels often are parts of a series, not surprising since, life ends (its final change) and art ends (its final satisfaction) while escape —never quite satisfying enough—is condemned to tread over and over again the same barren ground.[2]

There is only one direct criticism of Tolkien in this passage—"the fixity of Lewis' and *Tolkien's* characters"—and it may be that Russ would not apply her criticisms of Lewis to Tolkien, though her use of the term *Secondary Universe* suggests an overall application to Tolkien of her remarks. At any rate, other critics have condemned Tolkien in just the terms in which Russ criticizes Lewis: "dreadful predictability," "nobles stay noble," and so on. Russ's rather bad-tempered outburst was occasioned by the many bad imitations of Tolkien, and certainly it is a just criticism of some of these. But when Tolkien is criticized in these terms, one wonders if the critics have actually *read* the stories, or have been so blinded by their presuppositions that they see only what they want to see. As C. S. Lewis points out (speaking of science fiction as well as fantasy):

It is very dangerous to write about a kind of literature you hate. Hatred obscures all distinctions. I don't like detective stories and therefore all detective stories look much alike to me: if I wrote about them I should therefore infallibly write drivel. Criticism of kinds, as distinct from criticism of works, cannot of course be avoided. . . . But it is, I think the most subjective and least reliable type of criticism. Above all, it should not masquerade as criticism of individual works. Many reviews are useless because, while purporting to condemn the book, they only reveal the reviewer's dislike of the kind to which it belongs. Let bad tragedies be censured by those who love tragedy, and bad detective stories by those who love the detective story. Then we shall learn their real faults. Otherwise we shall find epics blamed for not being novels, farces for not being high comedies, novels by James for lacking the swift action of Smollett. Who wants to hear a particular claret abused by a fanatical teetotaller, or a particular woman by a confirmed misogynist. . . .

How anyone can think this form illegitimate or contemptible passes my understanding. It may very well be convenient not to call such things novels. If you prefer, call them a very special form of novels. Either way, the conclusion will be much the same: they are to be tried by their own rules. It is absurd to condemn them because they do not often display any deep or sensitive characterization. They oughtn't to. It is a fault if they do. Wells' Cavor and Bedford have rather too much than too little character. Every good writer knows that the more unusual the scenes and events of his story are, the slighter, the more ordinary, the more typical his persons should be. Hence Gulliver is a commonplace little man and Alice a commonplace little girl. If they had been more remarkable they would have wrecked their books. The Ancient Mariner himself is a very ordinary man. To tell how odd things struck odd people is to have an oddity too much: he who is to see strange sights must not himself be strange. He ought to be as nearly as possible Everyman or Anyman. Of course, we must not confuse slight or typical characterization with impossible or unconvincing characterization. Falsification of character will always spoil a story. But character can apparently be reduced, simplified, to almost any extent with wholly satisfactory results. The greater ballads are an instance.

Of course, a given reader may be (some readers seem to be) interested in nothing else in the world except detailed studies of complex human personalities. If so, he has a good reason for not reading those kinds of work which neither demand nor admit it. He has no reason for condemning them, and indeed no qualification for speaking of them at all. We must not allow the novel of manners to give laws to all literature: let it rule its own domain. We must not listen to Pope's maxim about the proper study of mankind. The proper study of man is everything. The proper study of man as artist is everything which gives a foothold to the imagination and the passions.[3]

These are fairly clearly the standards Russ is using in criticizing heroic fantasy: her dictum that "fiction's only real subject is the changes that occur in human beings" is simply a more plausible version, because it is a less specific version, of the demand that fantasy copy the kind of novel that is currently favored by the critics. Not surprisingly, defenders of fantasy have counterattacked by pointing out the narrow concerns of the modern novel as compared with the whole range of the history of literature: it is the "mainstream" or "mundane" novel that fails to live up to the full possibilities of literature.

If all of Joanna Russ's criticism were ideological disagreement disguised as aesthetic evaluation, her criticism would be useless, for ideas can only be refuted by argument or evidence. Russ's criticism is often very valuable when it does not involve her prejudices, and is sometimes illuminating even when it does. Thus, for example, her idea that the witch in the Narnia stories is seen as an evil character *because* she is a "proud, independent and therefore wicked woman" is absurd to anyone who has read the Narnia stories without Russ's particular opinions. It is a fact that sexist stereotypes do occur in science fiction. But Russ's remarks show that she sees certain faults she is sensitive to whether they are present or not. This does not mean that they are not faults, only that Russ is an unreliable guide to this sort of fault; falsely crying "wolf" too often destroys one's credibility when real wolves are at the flock.

The moral of all this is that we must not expect moral conflicts in Tolkien's fiction to be expressed in the same way that they would be expressed in realistic modern fiction. There will be less psychological probing, more use of the symbolic and archetypal. But anyone who can talk of the "fixity" of Tolkien's characters is simply ignoring a massive body of evidence: Boromir's fall and repentance, Gollum's almost-repentance, Frodo's genuine temptations and eventual moral failure. Aragorn, who seems to be the target of the burlesque quoted by Russ, faces no particular moral crisis in the story, but not every character in every story need change and grow in that story. Actually Aragorn's growing respect for Frodo and Sam and his gentle handling of Éowen's love for him provide some growth and development in his character, even though his main function is to be the archetypal "Returned King."

Another, even more perceptive, writer and critic of science fiction and fantasy, Ursula LeGuin, asks whether in-depth characterization can occur in science fiction and fantasy. In her essay "Science Fiction and Mrs. Brown," LeGuin cites Virginia Woolf's dictum that "all novels deal with character . . . it is to express character that the form of the novel . . . has been evolved." Following Woolf, LeGuin calls the real, ordinary person who ought to inhabit the novel Mrs. Brown and goes on as follows:

If any field of literature has no, can have no Mrs. Browns in it, it is fantasy —straight fantasy the modern descendant of folktale, fairy tale and myth. These genres deal with archetypes not with characters. The very essence of Elfland is that Mrs. Brown can't get there—not unless she is changed, changed utterly, into an old mad witch or a fair young princess or a loathly Worm.

But who is this character, then, who really looks very like Mrs. Brown, except that he has furry feet: a short, thin, tired-looking fellow wearing a gold ring on a chain around his neck, and heading rather disconsolately eastward, on foot? I think you know his name.

Actually, I will not argue hard in defense of Frodo Baggins as a genuine, fully developed moralistic character. . . . If you put Frodo together into one piece with Sam, and with Gollum, and with Sméagol—and they fit together into one piece—you get, indeed, a complex and fascinating character. But as traditional myths and folk tales break the complex conscious daylight personality down into its archetypical unconscious dreamtime components, Mrs. Brown becoming a princess, a toad, a worm, a witch, a child—so Tolkien in his wisdom broke Frodo into four: Frodo, Sam, Sméagol and Gollum, perhaps five, counting Bilbo. Gollum is probably the best character in the book because he gets two of the components, Sméagol and Gollum, or as Sam calls them, Slinker and Stinker. Frodo himself is only a quarter or fifth of himself. Yet even so he is something new to fantasy: a vulnerable, limited rather unpredictable hero, who finally fails at his own quest—fails at the very end of it, and has to have it accomplished for him by his mortal enemy, Gollum, who is, however, his kinsman, his brother, in fact himself. . . . And who then goes home to the Shire, very much as Mrs. Brown would do if she had the chance, but then he has to go on, leave home, make the voyage out, in fact die— something fantasy heroes never do and allegories are incapable of doing.

I shall never cease to wonder at the critics who find Tolkien a "simple" writer. What marvelously simple minds they must have![4]

LeGuin does not have a simple mind: she is able to appreciate the virtues of those she disagrees with. Her own fantasy world of Earthsea is based on a Taoist idea of "Balance," and she has described herself as anti-Christian. The third book of her Earthsea trilogy is based on the humanist idea that hope for immortality, for life after death, spoils both life and art—an idea that Tolkien would strongly reject, as we will see. But LeGuin can make the distinction, which many other writers and critics have lost sight of, between ideological disagreement and critical judgment of a work of art as art.

Probably one question on which many modern critics of Tolkien are in fundamental disagreement with him is the question of the proper *use* of free will. Grant, for the moment, that we *are* free: what use should we make of our freedom? Tolkien says that his characters (and, by implication, ourselves) have a mission to carry out, a destiny. In *The Lord of the Rings,* only hints are given as to the source of this destiny. In the more explicitly theological and mythological *Silmarillion,* it is made clear that our destinies are given to us by God, and that our choice is whether to freely accept those destinies and be happy or to reject those destinies and be unhappy. This is made very clear in the story of Fëanor, the creator of the Silmarils.

Fëanor is the son of one of the great Elvenkings, Finwë. He is the greatest craftsman of the Elves, and his supreme work of craftsmanship is the creation of the three great jewels, the Silmarils, into which Fëanor puts some of the light of the two great Trees that give light to the Blessed Realm.

Fëanor is a person of tremendous force and eloquence, as well as being a great craftsman. We are told that giving birth to him so exhausts his mother, Míriel, that she goes away from her family to seek rest and eventually goes into a deathlike trance, her body incorrupt, but her spirit in the Halls of Mandos, where Elvish spirits await reincarnation. Finwë responds to this by an almost obsessive love for his son but eventually remarries and has other children, arousing Fëanor's jealousy. It is a surprisingly intricate piece of psychological motivation for Fëanor's later actions, given the high mythological style of *The Silmarillion.*

There is also a more "mythological" kind of motivation for what follows. Melkor has been defeated by the Valar, and after a long term of imprisonment, he pretends repentance and is given his freedom. He goes among the Elves spreading suspicion and distrust of the Valar, suggesting subtly that the Valar want to exploit the Elves and keep them subservient. At last Melkor, in alliance with a great spiderlike creature, attacks the Blessed Land at a time of festival when everyone is off guard. Melkor and his ally destroy the Two Trees that give light to the Blessed Land and escape. As they leave the Blessed Land, Melkor kills Finwë and steals the Silmarils, but neither Fëanor nor the Valar realizes this at first.

Since the Silmarils contain some of the Light of the Two Trees, they can be used to repair the damage done by Melkor. Yavanna, one of the Valar, tells the others:

"The Light of the Trees has passed away and lives now only in the Silmarils of Fëanor. Foresighted was he! Even for those mightiest under Ilúvatar there is some work which they may accomplish once, and once only. The Light of the Trees I brought into being, and within Eä I can do so never again. Yet had I but a little of that light I could recall life to the Trees, ere their roots decay: and then our hurts should be healed and the Malice of Melkor confounded."[5]

Fëanor now has an opportunity to be the means by which a great harm is healed, just as Frodo has later. He is not even required to struggle and suffer as Frodo will have to, partly because this is only the beginning of the harm, and if it can be healed immediately, it can be healed without great toil and suffering. However, it requires a tremendous sacrifice on Fëanor's part, as he tells the Valar:

But Fëanor spoke then and cried bitterly, "For the less even as for the greater there is some deed he may accomplish but once only; and in that deed his heart shall rest. It may be that I can unlock my jewels, but never again shall I make their like: and if I must break them I shall break my heart."[6]

Moved by his feeling of possessiveness for the jewels and by the memory of Melkor's whispers that the Valar want to exploit and control the Elves, Fëanor refuses to give up the Silmarils. Then the message comes that his father is slain and the Silmarils stolen. "The Silmarils had passed away and all one it may seem whether Fëanor had said yea or nay to Yavanna: yet had he said yea at the first before the tidings came . . . it may be that his after deeds would have been other than they were."[7]

Maddened with rage and grief for his father, Fëanor now uses his eloquence and force of character to persuade a great many of the Elves to leave the Blessed Land and return to Middle-earth, both to pursue Melkor and the Silmarils and to get away from the Valar and their rule. To make his way back to Middle-earth without delays that might cause him to lose his hold on his followers, Fëanor takes desperate measures:

he and his followers demand ships of a group of seafaring Elves; when they refuse, Fëanor's followers kill many of them and steal the ships. Later Fëanor abandons some of his less enthusiastic followers when the ships will not carry all of his group. Fëanor himself eventually dies in an attack on Melkor, and his spirit remains in the Halls of Mandos. His sons have sworn a terrible oath to recover the Silmarils, and this oath will cause trouble, treachery, and strife for long ages in Middle-earth.

The story of Fëanor brings together many themes we have discussed previously. Like Niggle, Fëanor is faced with a choice between the needs of others and his own greatest work of art. Like Frodo, Fëanor is asked to make a sacrifice for the good of others. We have said that the greatest temptation of the Elves is to a sort of avarice or possessiveness and that they can also be moved by pride, envy, and anger. Possessiveness for the Silmarils, envy of the Valar, anger at his father's death, and a pride that will not admit his own limitations all go into Fëanor's fall.

Tolkien plainly means to say that Fëanor made the wrong choice, showing how it led to disaster for himself and for those who follow him, how the first evil choice led to murder and treachery and other crimes. Unlike Frodo, Fëanor refuses his destiny. He never learns the lesson Niggle learns—that art must take a second place to morality.

However, there is a tendency in modern thought that would be on the side of Fëanor. This tendency often goes with the denial of any powers higher than the human, so the issue is not always as clear-cut as in Fëanor's case. Fëanor is being asked to return the fire that *he* took from Yavanna's Trees, repay the debt that he and the other Elves owe to the Valar for teaching and protection. The modern who does not believe in God will be consistent in feeling no gratitude or obligation for his or her gifts and talents. But many moderns would want to say that even if God does exist it does not change the situation: we must still be masters of our own destinies.

Even those who disagree with this view might have some reservations about the way in which Ilúvatar is depicted in Tolkien as never directly communicating with the Elves, ruling them through the Valar, who are God's representatives or regents in Arda, the created world. A rather similar situation is depicted in C. S. Lewis's *Out of the Silent*

Planet, where the three embodied Martian races are ruled by disembodied angelic beings, the Eldila. Both Tolkien and Lewis might have been influenced to some extent by passages in Saint Paul's epistles in which the apostle says that, until the coming of Christ, God dealt with us through angels.

Lewis's Eldila seem always to be wise and in the right, at least so far as we see them revealed in the story. Interestingly, Tolkien seems to sometimes suggest that his Valar are not always right and sometimes make unwise decisions. In a passage early in *The Silmarillion,* the Valar decide to summon the Elves from Middle-earth to Valinor, the Blessed Land, in order to teach them and protect them from the attacks of Melkor.

Then again the Valar were gathered in council, and they were divided in debate. For some, and of those Ulmo was the chief, held that the Quendi [Elves] should be left free to walk as they would in Middle-earth, and with their gifts of skill to order all the lands and heal their hurts. But the most part feared for the Quendi in the dangerous world amid the deceits of the starlight dusk; and they were filled moreover with the love of the beauty of the Elves and desired their fellowship. At the last, therefore, the Valar summoned the Quendi to Valinor, there to be gathered at the knees of the Powers in the light of the Trees for ever; and Mandos broke his silence, saying: "So it is doomed." From this summons came many woes that afterwards befell.[8]

This is a problem faced by every parent and to some extent by every teacher: how much to guide and guard those under our tutelage, how much to protect them from dangers that we can see better than they. Tolkien at least hints that the Valar were being overprotective and that it might have been better to leave the Elves in Middle-earth to learn and grow on their own, with such help and protection as the Valar could give them there.

It is perhaps not too fanciful to see Tolkien here making use of his experiences as a Catholic. Since the Second Vatican Council, the Catholic church has increasingly tried to give more responsibility and freedom to laypeople. But for most of Tolkien's life the church was perhaps too paternalistic and overprotective. In fact, there were even similarities in method: Catholic leaders in England and elsewhere tended to try to create a separate culture, with Catholic schools, Catholic newspapers, Catholic publishing houses, and so on. If it had been possible to summon all Catholics to a country of their own where they would be taught and watched over by the hierarchy, that solution would probably have appealed to some Catholic bishops!

Tolkien, as a convinced Catholic engaged in education at Oxford and involved in many ways with the non-Catholic world, could see the dangers of this "ghettoization" of Catholic culture, as could many Catholic intellectuals during this period. In a letter to his son Michael, Tolkien comments on some of the changes in Catholicism during his lifetime:

"Trends" in the Church are . . . serious especially to those accustomed to find in it a solace and a "pax" in times of temporal trouble, and not just another arena of strife and change. But imagine the experience of those born (as I) between the Golden and Diamond Jubilee of [Queen] Victoria . . . "my church" was not intended by Our Lord to be static or remain in perpetual childhood but to be a living organism (likened to a plant), which develops and changes in externals by the interaction of its bequeathed divine life and history—the particular circumstances of the world in which it is set. . . .

I find myself in sympathy with these movements that are strictly "ecumenical," that is concerned with other groups and churches that call themselves (and often are) "Christian." . . . An increase in "charity" is an enormous gain. . . . There are dangers (of course) but a Church militant cannot afford to shut up all its soldiers in a fortress. It had as bad effects on the Maginot Line.[9]

Whether or not Tolkien had this Catholic situation in mind when he wrote of the protectiveness of the Valar, he did depict them as gathering the Elves into a sort of fortress, a static defense like the Maginot Line in World War I. And just as the Maginot Line was rendered useless by bold, fast-moving attacks by the Germans, so Melkor is able to successfully attack suddenly and with surprise (after a period of softening up the Elves by propaganda—another parallel to German tactics in the two world wars).

It is also possible that Tolkien was especially aware of the dangers of overprotectiveness because of his experience with Father Francis Morgan, the Catholic priest who was his guardian after the death of Tolkien's mother. Though quite liberal about Tolkien's education,

Father Francis was more protective about his personal life, and when Tolkien met Edith Bratt and seemed likely to make an early and seemingly imprudent marriage, Father Francis exacted from Tolkien a promise not to communicate at all with Edith until his twenty-first birthday. Because of his gratitude to and respect for the priest, Tolkien made and kept this promise, but it caused him a great deal of unhappiness, which he must to some extent have attributed to overprotectiveness on the part of Father Francis.

Tolkien's views about morality and religion, the proper use of free will, and the purpose of human life are expressed very indirectly in his fiction; occasionally, in letters to his children or to close friends, he makes his views more explicit. In a letter to the daughter of his friend and publisher Rayner Unwin, Tolkien says that

morals should be a guide to our human purposes, the conduct of our lives: (a) the way in which our individual talents can be developed without waste or misuse; and (b) without injuring our kindred or interfering with their development. (Beyond this and higher lies self-sacrifice for love.) . . .

Those who believe in a personal God, Creator, do not think that the Universe is itself worshipful, though devoted study of it may be one of the ways of honoring Him. And while as living creatures we are (in part) within it and part of it, our ideas of God and ways of expressing them will be largely derived from contemplating the world about us. (Though there is revelation addressed to all men and to particular persons.)

So it may be said that the chief purpose of life, for any one of us is to increase according to our capacity our knowledge of God by all the means we have and to be moved by it to praise and thanks.[10]

Tolkien's own form of "praise and thanks" was to create a "secondary world" that develops certain "themes" of the real world and enables us to better appreciate the world made by God. As he says in the essay "On Fairy Stories":

Fantasy is built out of the Primary World, but a good craftsman loves his material, and has knowledge and feeling for clay, stone and wood which only the art of making can give. By the forging of Gram cold iron was revealed; by the making of Pegasus horses were enabled; in the Trees of the Sun and Moon root and stock, flower and fruit are manifested in glory.

And actually fairy-stories deal largely, or (the better ones) mainly with simple or fundamental things, untouched by Fantasy, but these simplicities are made all the more luminous by their setting. For the story maker who allows himself to be "free with" Nature can be her lover, not her slave. It was in fairy stories that I first divined the potency of the words, and the wonder of the things, such as stone and wood, and iron; tree and grass; house and fire; bread and wine.[11]

10. The Sudden Joyous Turn

Earlier I quoted a letter in which Tolkien says that the real theme of *The Lord of the Rings* is death and immortality. This statement by the author of the story must be taken seriously, but it is surprising and at first we are inclined to resist accepting it. Very few of the characters die in the story. There is little talk of death or immortality, and there is certainly no description of or reflection on a life after death. Once we start thinking along these lines, however, we can see that there is perhaps more emphasis on death than we thought at first: the Barrow-wights, the Dead Aragorn leads from the Paths of the Dead, the dead Elves and Men Frodo and Sam see in the Dead Marshes, and even the Black Riders are all reminders of death. Boromir, Denethor, Théoden, and Gollum all die in scenes important to the plot; Gandalf and Frodo both seem to have died at key points in the action. Furthermore, some of the important images in the story could be taken as death images: the blasted land of Mordor, the destruction of the Ring, the passage over the Western Sea.

About immortality, however, Tolkien at first seems to have almost nothing to say. The Elves are immortal so long as the world lasts, and this is an important fact about them. The Blessed Land, Valinor, is also called the Undying Land. The wizards and Sauron can be "unbodied" as Saruman and Sauron are, but they cannot really be killed. This seems at first to be about all the use that Tolkien makes of the idea of immortality. But we should be aware by now that Tolkien is a writer who achieves many of his most important effects by indirection, and what is most important to him is often not stated but underlies the whole story. As he says of religion, "the religious element is absorbed into the story and the symbolism."[1]

To see what Tolkien is trying to do with the themes of death and immortality, I will try to extract some general themes from Tolkien's letters and other comments on his work and then show how they are "absorbed into the story and the symbolism." I will then contrast Tolkien's view of immortality with others embodied in fantasy literature, the much more explicit treatment in C. S. Lewis and the anti-immortality view of Ursula LeGuin. We can thus appreciate in better perspective the immortality in *The Lord of the Rings* and its importance.

The first theme I can draw from Tolkien's discussions of his work is the contrast of true and false immortality. The Ring itself is, of course, one of the most important symbols in *The Lord of the Rings*. We are explicitly told by Gandalf that the Ring gives a *sort* of immortality, but not true immortality. "A mortal, Frodo, who keeps one of the Great Rings does not die, but he does not grow or obtain more life, he merely continues until at last every minute is a weariness."[2] Both Bilbo and Gollum are spoken of as being "stretched out," "thinned out" by the long life that is given to them by the Ring; the metaphor is that of making something longer not by adding more material to it but by stretching it so that its existing material covers more area but is less substantial. The suggestion is that as the *quantity* of life increases, the *quality* decreases, "until at last every minute is a weariness."

There is an underlying idea of a normal or natural "size" or life span here: compressing the normal span of a life into a very brief period would be as bad as stretching it out to a too-long period. It is an idea that seems in many ways natural and intuitive: we speak of someone who dies young as being "cut off" prematurely, and old people sometimes feel that they have lived beyond their proper span. Interestingly, we sometimes speak of someone who lived hard and died young as having crammed a whole lifetime into a few brief years.

The idea can have many sources: the Greek ideal of the golden mean, of "nothing in excess," and the Old Testament idea of "three score and ten" as a proper human life span. In fact, the familiar quotation goes on to say "and if a man lives on beyond this by reason of strength his life grows weary." Humans of the Old Blood (with an Elvish mixture) and even Hobbits have a longer life span than this, but still a limited one. Bilbo is considered respectably old at the age of III, and one of the Hobbits most famous for age died at 130. Tolkien himself died at 81, and his last years, though happy in many ways, were sometimes wearisome to him.

It is clear enough what Tolkien would be inclined to say about modern advances in medical science that extend a bare existence for old people with almost everything that makes life worth living gone. But there is an additional moral to be drawn from Tolkien's idea of false immortality. Other things besides individual lives may have a natural span, which it is unwise to extend. The Elvish enclaves of Rivendell and Lothlórien have been preserved and protected by the power of two of the three Rings of Power that belong to the Elves. Those who wear them, Elrond and Galadriel, are Elves and so naturally immortal, so even if the rings they wear extend life this would not matter to them. But the very existence of the strongholds maintained by use of the Rings may be an unwise attempt to extend the natural span of Elvish presence on Middle-earth.

The coming age, we are told, is to be the Age of Men, and perhaps it has or should have already begun. Certainly the defeat of Sauron would have been more difficult without the Elves—Elrond's wisdom, Galadriel's gifts. But would it have been impossible? The forces that battle Sauron are mainly under the command of Aragorn; the real defeat of Sauron is accomplished by Frodo, Sam, and even Gollum, all Hobbits. In his letters, Tolkien clears up a point that was not clear in *The Lord of the Rings:* "The Hobbits are, of course, really meant to be a branch of the specifically *human* race (not Elves or Dwarves)."[3] Thus, the major part of the defeat of Sauron is due to humans, with the help of Gandalf, the messenger of the Valar. So it cannot be said that the Elves *had* to stay in Middle-earth to defeat Sauron.

There are many ways in which we might apply this moral more mundanely: there is a tendency in all of us to cling to the familiar and try to extend things in our life beyond their natural span, whether this takes the form of a young person trying to overextend the period of irresponsible youth or an older person clinging to a job when he or she should retire to make place for younger people.

The second contrast Tolkien draws is the contrast of physical immortality with a life after physical death. As we have seen, the Elves are immortal so long as Earth lasts: they do not die naturally, and if they die by violence or accident, they can come back from the Halls of Mandos re-embodied. From the language used about human deaths, it is clear that the person is thought of as continuing to exist, but that nothing is known or believed about what happens to the person. So humans do not know what will happen to them after death, but the Elves do not know what will happen to them after the end of the physical world.

In his essay "On Fairy Stories," Tolkien says that one of the purposes of fantasy is consolation, and at first glance this rather agnostic view of life after death does not seem to be especially consoling. And in one sense it is not: it does not offer easy reassurance or emotional consolation. But underlying Tolkien's writing on the subject is a firm belief that there *is* something after death and that we can trust in the wisdom and goodness of God to ensure that whatever comes after death will be not only just but generous. As a religious poster I once saw put it: "To believe in God is to know that all the rules are fair and there will be wonderful surprises."

This rather austere assurance that we will continue to exist after death and that we can trust in God for what happens to us is all that Tolkien offers in his stories. It is illuminating to contrast his work with that of his friend C. S. Lewis and his admirer Ursula LeGuin in the way in which life after death is treated.

Lewis in several of his works gives glimpses or hints of an afterlife. Perhaps the most detailed picture he gives is that in his children's fantasy *The Last Battle,*[4] one of the *Chronicles of Narnia.* A considerable portion of the story is concerned with the after-death experiences of the protagonists of the story. They meet old friends who have died before them, witness a Last Judgment scene, experience extreme happiness, peace, and exhilaration and at the end of the story meet and embrace Aslan, the Christ-figure of the Narnia stories. Many people, both children and adults, find this story extremely encouraging and consoling. When I read the story to two of my sons when they were quite young I afterward heard one say to the other, "You don't need to be afraid of dying if it's like it is in the Narnia stories." Even after repeated readings, I still find the last scene of the book so poignant that it brings tears to my eyes.

Tolkien is on record as not liking the Narnia stories, and I think that he might feel that drawing a fictional picture of the afterlife was offering the wrong kind of consolation. If "eye has not seen, nor ear heard, nor has it entered into the heart of man what glories God has prepared for those who love Him," then why attempt to describe what is by definition indescribable? I think Tolkien might take a position on this rather like the position he took on illustrations for fairy stories: "the visible representation of the fantastic image is technically too easy; the hand tends to outrun the mind, even to overthrow it. Silliness and morbidity are frequent results."[5]

It is not certain that Tolkien would have applied this kind of stricture to attempts to picture a life after death in fiction, but one interesting piece of collateral evidence is that another book of Lewis's that Tolkien expressed a dislike for is *Letters to Malcolm*, in which Lewis presents some nonfictional speculations on life after death.

Of course Tolkien pictures a sort of life after death in "Leaf by Niggle," as we saw in Chapter 2, but the purpose there is allegorical and moralistic; the picture is not presented for "consolation." In fact, Lewis would have agreed with Tolkien that using stories about heaven for one kind of consolation is a moral and religious mistake. As he says in the book *A Grief Observed*, which he wrote after his wife's death:

Talk to me about the truth of religion and I'll listen gladly. Talk to me about the duty of religion and I'll listen submissively. But don't come talking to me about the consolation of religion, or I shall suspect you don't understand.

Unless, of course, you can literally believe all that stuff about family reunions "on the farther shore" pictured in entirely earthly terms. But that is all unscriptural, all out of bad hymns and lithographs. There's not a word of it in the Bible. And it rings false. We *know* it can't be like that. Reality never repeats. The exact same thing is never taken away and given back.[6]

One possible objection to Lewis's imaginative pictures of heaven in *The Last Battle* is that he is there depicting heaven in "entirely earthly terms," just what he says "rings false" in the passage just quoted. I think that Lewis might have replied that his fantasy picture of the afterlife is not intended for primary belief: that it is an attempt to express a religious truth in imaginative terms. Many things in life, such as deep romantic love, may be in some sense "inexpressible," but it is legitimate to try to express them as best we can.

At the other extreme from Lewis we have the criticism of the idea of immortality in Ursula LeGuin's book *The Farthest Shore*. The basic premise of the book is that the desire for personal immortality is selfish and destructive; in reaching for immortality, we poison and destroy both ordinary life and art. As the Archmage, Ged, says in the story:

"You will die. You will not live forever. Nor will any man or thing. Nothing is immortal. But only to us is it given to know that we must die. And that is a great gift: the gift of selfhood. For we have only what we know we must lose, what we are willing to lose. . . . That selfhood which is our torment and our treasure and our humanity does not endure. It changes; it is gone, a wave on the sea. Would you have the sea grow still and the tides cease to save one wave, to save yourself? Would you give the craft of your hands and the passion of your heart and the light of sunrise and sunset, to buy safety for yourself—safety forever? . . . That is the message. . . . By denying life, you may deny death and live forever!—And this is the message I do not hear . . . for I will not hear it. I will not take the counsel of despair."[7]

Of course a story is not an argument (though LeGuin does sometimes stop the action of *The Farthest Shore* for Ged's arguments). But the greatest difficulty with LeGuin's position is the justification of the idea *(a)* that by wanting immortality we somehow damage other people or nature (have the sea grow still . . . to save one wave) and *(b)* that to have immortality we must deny life. The justification of these ideas in the story is in terms of the idea of a cosmic Balance that can be disturbed by actions that are "against nature." Why is immortality "against nature"? Because, Ged says:

"There are two . . . that make one: the world and the shadow, the light and the dark. The two poles of the Balance. Life arises out of death, death rises out of life: in being opposite they yearn to each other, they give birth to each other and are forever reborn. And with them all is reborn, the flower of the apple tree, the light of the stars. In life is death; in death is rebirth. What then is life without death? Life unchanging, everlasting, eternal?—What is it but death—death without rebirth?"[8]

Taken out of poetic language, the basic accusation is that refusal of death is refusal of change. But for Tolkien, as we have seen, refusal of change is *false* immortality. It is certainly true that if plants, animals, and so on did not die there would be no room for new plants and animals. If human beings did not die they might even gradually increase and multiply and overcrowd the earth or else stop having children and deny new life. But what "balance" would be disturbed by an immortal race like Tolkien's Elves who increased very slowly if at all (we hear very little about birth or children among the Elves) and who lived as long as the world endured? Why could not such a race learn and grow and change without death?

Of course humans are not a race of this kind: we do die and perhaps need to die. But this is the second part of Tolkien's thesis: humans should not seek for physical immortality. The kind of immortality that LeGuin objects to in her story is at worst false immortality (denial of change, stretching life beyond natural limits) and at best physical immortality (continued physical existence in this world). In fact, in the story LeGuin pictures the immortality that Ged objects to as extremely unpleasant, rather like the false immortality given by the Ring.

But how does anything LeGuin says constitute an objection to life after death? Why is it necessarily life-denying to believe that after death there is a new life, a continued personal existence that involves unending growth in love and knowledge? Afterlife as continued growth is expressed by the metaphor that both Lewis (in *The Great Divorce*) and Tolkien (in "Leaf by Niggle") use: the afterlife as a continued *journey* further and further in to "the mountains" that symbolize new "peaks" of experience.

One answer to this challenge is implicit in LeGuin's story: that by thinking of ourselves as surviving after death we are thinking of ourselves as superior to nature rather than as part of it. A character in the story who seeks the kind of immortality that LeGuin condemns says, "I have seen death now and I will not accept it. Let all stupid nature go its stupid course but I am a man, better than nature, above nature. I will not go that way, I will not cease to be myself!"[9]

But of course if we accept a Christian world view like Tolkien's, we *are* superior to nonhuman nature; Nature is our sister, not our mother or mistress. As Tolkien said in a letter quoted previously, "Those who believe in a personal God, Creator, do not think that the Universe is itself worshipful."[10] He goes on to say in the same letter, "in moments of exaltation we may call on all created things to join in our chorus, speaking on their behalf, as is done in Psalm 148 and in the Song of the Three Children in Daniel II. PRAISE THE LORD . . . all mountains and halls, all orchards and forests, all things that creep and birds on the wing."[11]

This of course is the fundamental philosophical difference between LeGuin and Tolkien. He accepts a Christian view of the universe; she accepts a view that humans are only part of nature and cannot transcend it, a view that has been called "Taoist" by some commentators on LeGuin. Naturally, she will object to our setting ourselves above nature, and naturally Tolkien will not. But "nature" can have many senses (for example, what we are accustomed to or do not find surprising, as when I said "Naturally, LeGuin will . . . "). The Christian view certainly does not make humans superior to "total reality," which includes God and angels as well as subhuman nature (animals, plants, lifeless matter). On the Christian view, humans occupy a rather modest position in the hierarchy even of created beings, with responsibility and respect both "upward" and "downward."

There seems to be no reason why a Christian view should be antiecological or antinature (Tolkien's Elves are physically immortal beings who have a special care of and feeling for nature: and for Tolkien the Elves are an idealization of one part of human nature). Why should Tolkien's view be less valid or convincing than LeGuin's? I think that she might reply that historically Christianity has been life-denying, has praised celibacy and asceticism, has led to the idea that humans are "lords of creation" and can loot it for their own purposes. But as Christian theologians have pointed out, the attitude that we can do as we like with nature by no means follows from Christianity.[12] And celibacy and asceticism were praised because they involved giving up things good in themselves for love of God and to serve our fellow humans. Of course there have been antimatter, antilife views, such as Manichaeism, Catharism, Jansenism, but these were heresies, not mainstream Christianity.

We find, then, that Tolkien's picture of life after death, though not explicitly consolatory like that of Lewis, is far different from the antiimmortality view of LeGuin. Perhaps we should ask, then, what Tolkien means by "consolation" in fantasy. If death is "the gift of Ilúvatar," if his characters go into death hoping but without explicit assurances, what is the "consolation" that Tolkien's fantasies contain?

Here is what Tolkien says in "On Fairy Stories":

There is the oldest and deepest desire, the Great Escape, the Escape from Death. Fairy stories provide many examples and modes of this—which might be called the genuine *escapist* or (I would say) *fugitive* spirit. But so do other stories, (notably those of scientific inspiration) and so do other studies. Fairy stories are made by men, not by fairies. The Human-stories of the elves are doubtless full of the Escape from Deathlessness. But our stories cannot be expected always to rise above our common level. They often do. Few lessons are taught more clearly in them than the burden of that kind of immortality or rather endless serial living to which the "fugitive" would fly. . . . But the "consolation" of fairy-tales has another aspect than the imaginative satisfaction of ancient desires. Far more important is the Consolation of the Happy Ending. Almost I would venture to assert that all complete fairy-stories must have it. At least I would say that Tragedy is the true form of Drama, its highest function; but the opposite is true of Fairy-story. Since we do not appear to have a word that expresses this opposite—I will call it Eucatastrophe. The *eucatastrophic* tale is the true form of fairy-tale, and its highest function.

The consolation of fairy-stories is the joy of the happy ending: or more correctly of the good catastrophe, the sudden joyous "turn" (for there is no true end to any fairy-tale): this joy is one which fairy-stories can produce supremely well, it is not essentially "escapist" or "fugitive." In its fairy-tale —or otherworld—setting it is a sudden and miraculous grace: never to be counted on to recur. It does not deny the existence of *dyscatastrophe,* of sorrow and failure: the possibility of these is necessary to the joy of deliverance; it denies (in the face of much evidence, if you will) universal final defeat and so far is *evangelium,* giving a fleeting glimpse of Joy. Joy beyond the walls of the world, poignant as grief.[13]

This Joy does exist in fairy tales, does exist in Tolkien's tales. But does it exist in reality? Tolkien goes on to say, in the epilogue to "On Fairy Stories":

The peculiar quality of the "joy" in successful Fantasy can . . . be explained as a sudden glimpse of the underlying reality or truth. It is not only a "consolation" for the sorrow of this world, but a satisfaction, and an answer to the question "Is it true?" The answer to the question I gave at first was (quite rightly) "If you have built your little world well, yes: it is true in that world." That is enough for the artist (or the artist part of the artist). But in the "eucatastrophe" we see in a brief vision that the answer may be greater—it may be a far off gleam or echo of *evangelism* in the real world. . . .

The Gospels contain a fairy-story or a story of a larger kind which embraces all the essence of fairy-stories. They contain many marvels—peculiarly artistic, beautiful and moving: "Mythical" in their perfect, self-contained significance: and among these marvels is the greatest and most complete conceivable eucatastrophe. But this story has entered History and the primary world: the desire and aspiration of sub-creation has been raised to the fulfillment of Creation. The Birth of Christ is the eucatastrophe of Man's history. The Resurrection is the eucatastrophe of the Incarnation. This story begins and ends in joy. It has pre-eminently the "inner consistency of reality." There is no tale ever told that men would rather find was true, and none which so many sceptical men have accepted as true on its own merits. For the Art of it has the supremely convincing tone of Primary Art, that is, of Creation. To reject it leads to sadness or to wrath.[14]

This passage and those surrounding it is the key text for interpreting the heart of Tolkien's work. He was an artist who created a secondary world that has "the inner consistency of reality" for most, though not all, of his readers. But he was also a Christian, and his Christianity gave him the joy and vision that finds expression in his work. As he says in a letter to a sympathetic reader:

You speak of a "sanity and sanctity" in *The L. R.* "which is a power in itself." I was deeply moved. Nothing of the sort has been said to me before. But by a strange chance, just as I was beginning this letter, I had one from a man, who classified himself as "an unbeliever, or at best a man of belatedly and dimly dawning religious feeling . . . but you," he said, "create a world in which some sort of faith seems to be everywhere without a visible source, like light from an invisible lamp." I can only answer, Of his own sanity no man can securely judge. If sanctity inhabits his work or as a pervading light illumines it, it does not come from him but through him. And neither of you would perceive it in these terms unless it was with you also. Otherwise you would see and feel nothing, or (if some other spirit was present) you would be filled with contempt, nausea, hatred, "Leaves out of the elf-country, gah," "Lembas—dust and ashes, we don't eat that."[15]

The reference at the end of the passage is to the scene in *The Lord of the Rings* where Orcs are picking through Frodo's possessions after his capture and find the "lembas," the Elvish way-bread wrapped in leaves from Lórien. Their hatred of the Elves leads them to hate even leaves from "Elf-country," and the "lembas" that has sustained Frodo and Sam in their journey is to them only dust and ashes.

Not all of those who dislike and reject Tolkien's work do so in an Orcish spirit. No doubt some of Tolkien's critics hate God, and others merely hate Elves ("escapism," "no relation to real life"). Some critics, like LeGuin, who reject Tolkien's Christianity are large enough of spirit to accept Tolkien and his secondary world *as* a secondary world, an imagined universe that they believe does *not* reflect a reality in the primary world.

So those who do not accept Christianity will see Tolkien at best as an artist giving new imaginative expression to an outmoded view of the universe. Even as that, he is a counterexample to LeGuin's suggestion that desire for immortality "kills" art. (If another one were needed —almost all the great art ever created was created by believers in some form of religion.)

What of those who share Tolkien's religious beliefs? Some will reject his art because they are suspicious of reinterpretations of the Christian message in fantasy. But many will see him as in his own way an evangelist: someone who has expressed God's truth in a new form. It would not be intellectually responsible in these times to go back to the aesthetic religion discussed in Chapter 1, to accept something as true because it can be expressed beautifully. But it is highly reasonable in a wider sense of "reason" to consider more than linear, logical, argu-

mentative thinking in making a decision on matters of great importance. That a Christian philosophy has so often led to great beauty of
artistic expression is evidence. That in Christian art we find joy and in
nonreligious art we often find "anger and wrath" is evidence.

That those who love Tolkien tend to be nicer people than those who
hate him is even evidence. My own experience in "living with" Tolkien's books and letters during the period I have been writing this book
has been very positive: I admire Tolkien even more as a man and as
a writer than when I began to write about him, though I have loved
his work ever since I first read *The Hobbit* as a child. Not the least of
Tolkien's attractions is a certain Hobbit-like humility. In the letter we
just quoted, he remarks:

A few years ago I was visited in Oxford by a man . . . who said, "Of course
you don't suppose, do you, that you wrote that book yourself?"

Pure Gandalf! I was too well acquainted with G. to ask what he meant.
I think I said, "No, I don't suppose so any longer." I have never since been
able to suppose so. An alarming conclusion for an old philologist to draw
concerning his private amusement. But not one that should puff up any one
who considers the imperfections of "chosen instruments," and indeed what
sometimes seems their lamentable unfitness for the purpose.[16]

Whether Tolkien was a "chosen instrument" will depend on what
we think about whether there is One who chooses. Whether he was
"unfit" is a question only that Chooser can answer. Tolkien had his
faults. For example, his views of women were those of his time and
culture, and it is doubtful whether he ever had a woman friend he
regarded as fully his equal. (This may lie behind his objections to
C. S. Lewis's marriage to a woman who could only be approached as
an intellectual equal.) Tolkien was often dilatory, sometimes possessive,
about people and things and did not always live up to his own highest
standards. But which of us do? "Take him for all and all, this was a
man: we shall not see his like again."[17]

As for his work, that will live, I think, so long as men and women
and children have a "fascination with things Elvish." I can imagine an
overpuritanical Christian civilization that would have no room for
Tolkien, no room for anything except the pure gospel. I can much

more depressingly imagine mechanized, denaturized, Orcish unciviliza-
tion that would have no room for Tolkien or for his God, no room
for Hobbits, for Elves, for Ilúvatar. But we are not in so bad a state
yet, and while the light of Faerie still shines in this dark world, there
will be men and women and children to love Tolkien.

Not that it matters to him now. We can apply his own words about
Niggle to himself and his fellow creators of Christian fantasy. Such
fantasy

is proving very useful indeed . . . as a holiday and a refreshment. It is splendid
for convalescence, and not only for that, for many it is the best introduction
to the Mountains. It works wonders in some cases.[18]

And if Tolkien and his fellow Christian fantasists were told this,
perhaps their reaction would be that of Niggle and Parish: "They both
laughed. Laughed—the Mountains rang with it!"[19] Or, as Tolkien put
it in the essay "On Fairy Stories":

Story, fantasy, still go on and should go on. The Evangelium has not abrogated
legends, it has hallowed them, especially the "happy ending." The Christian
has still to work, with mind as well as body, to suffer, hope, and die, but he
may now perceive that all his bents and faculties have a purpose, which can
be redeemed. So great is the bounty with which he has been treated that he
may now, perhaps, fairly dare to hope that in Fantasy he may actually assist
in the effoliation and multiple enrichment of creation. All tales may come true,
and yet at the last, redeemed, they may be as like and as unlike the forms that
we give to them as Man, finally redeemed, will be like and unlike the fallen
that we know.[20]

Those of us who share Tolkien's faith may draw from these words
a happy hope: that Tolkien himself, long out of the Workhouse, is
preparing for us a happy realm amid the Father's many mansions; that
we who love his work may someday walk with him in the woods of
a redeemed Middle-earth: hear the Elvish voices sing and see the light
that never was on land or sea. And that will be a merry meeting.

Notes

Preface

1. C. S. Lewis, *That Hideous Strength* (New York: Macmillan, 1965), p. 7 of the paperback edition.
2. Richard L. Purtill, *Lord of the Elves and Eldils/Fantasy and Philosophy in C. S. Lewis and J. R. R. Tolkien* (Grand Rapids: Zondervan, 1973 [out of print]).
3. Richard L. Purtill, *C. S. Lewis's Case for the Christian Faith* (San Francisco: Harper & Row, 1982).
4. J. R. R. Tolkien, *The Silmarillion* (Boston: Houghton Mifflin, 1977); Humphrey Carpenter, *Tolkien: A Biography* (Boston: Houghton Mifflin, 1977); Humphrey Carpenter, ed., *The Letters of J. R. R. Tolkien* (Boston: Houghton Mifflin, 1981).
5. *Letters of J. R. R. Tolkien* (hereafter *Letters*), p. 424.

Chapter 1: The Dimensions of Myth

1. *Letters,* p. 144.
2. Ibid.
3. G. K. Chesterton, *The Everlasting Man* (New York: Doubleday, Image Books, 1955), p. 102.
4. Ibid., pp. 110, 112, 115.
5. Ibid., p. 173.
6. *Letters,* p. 194.
7. Ibid., p. 172.
8. Ibid., p. 246.
9. Ibid., p. 262.
10. C. S. Lewis, *An Experiment in Criticism* (New York: Cambridge University Press, 1961), pp. 43–44.
11. Ibid., p. 41.
12. *Letters,* p. 110.
13. E. V. Rieu, trans., *The Iliad* (Baltimore: Penguin Books, 1950), p. x.
14. Ibid., p. xvii.
15. Ibid., pp. xvii–xviii.
16. "On Fairy Stories," *The Tolkien Reader* (Boston: Houghton Mifflin, 1965), p. 24.
17. Ibid., p. 12.
18. Ibid., p. 16.
19. Ibid., p. 14.
20. Ibid., p. 72.

Chapter 2: Three Faces of Myth

1. J. R. R. Tolkien, *The Fellowship of the Ring* (New York: Ballantine Books, 1965), p. xi.
2. *Letters,* p. 257.
3. Ibid., p. 195.
4. Ibid., pp. 320–21.
5. W. H. Auden, *The Dyer's Hand* (New York: Knopf, 1962; New York: Vintage, 1968), p. 4.
6. Tolkien, "On Fairy Stories," p. 5.
7. Ibid., p. 26.

Chapter 3: Myth and Story

1. Poul Anderson, "Science Fiction and Science," in *Destinies,* vol. 1, no. 1, Oct.–Dec. 1978.
2. *Letters,* p. 172.
3. Ibid.
4. Ibid., p. 377.
5. Ibid., pp. 32–33.
6. Ibid., p. 342.
7. Ibid., p. 341.
8. Ibid., p. 349.
9. Carpenter, *Tolkien: A Biography,* p. 229.
10. Daniel Grotta, *J. R. R. Tolkien, Architect of Middle Earth* (Philadelphia: Running Press, 1978), pp. 123–27.
11. *Letters,* p. 367.
12. Carpenter, *Tolkein: A Biography*, p. 229.

Chapter 4: Hobbits and Heroism

1. *Letters,* p. 94.
2. Ibid., p. 236.
3. Ibid., p. 160.
4. J. R. R. Tolkien, *The Hobbit* (Boston: Houghton Mifflin, 1937), p. 27.
5. Ibid., p. 101.
6. Ibid.
7. Ibid., p. 167.
8. Ibid., pp. 226–27.
9. Ibid., p. 232.
10. 1 Corinthians 13:4–6, J. B. Phillips translation.
11. Tolkien, *The Hobbit,* pp. 30–31.
12. Ibid., p. 317.
13. *Letters,* p. 105.
14. Ibid., p. 161.
15. Tolkien, *The Fellowship of the Ring,* p. 150.
16. Ibid., p. 195.
17. *Letters,* p. 94.

18. Tolkien, *The Fellowship of the Ring,* pp. 519–20.
19. *Letters,* p. 110.
20. Ibid., p. 221.

Chapter 5: Beyond Heroism

1. J. R. R. Tolkien, *The Return of the King* (Boston: Houghton Mifflin, 1965), p. 274.
2. *Letters,* p. 330.
3. Tolkien, *The Return of the King,* p. 277.
4. *Letters,* p. 326.
5. Ibid., p. 234.
6. Tolkien, *The Return of the King,* p. 27.
7. Ibid., p. 35.
8. Ibid., p. 33.
9. Ibid., pp. 33–34.
10. Ibid., p. 158.
11. Tolkien, *The Fellowship of the Ring,* p. 340.
12. J. R. R. Tolkien, *The Two Towers* (Boston: Houghton Mifflin, 1965), p. 242.
13. Tolkien, *The Return of the King,* p. 368.
14. Ibid., p. 367.
15. Ibid., p. 352.
16. Ibid., p. 377.
17. G. K. Chesterton, *St. Francis of Assisi* (New York: Doubleday, Image Books, 1923), p. 112.
18. Tolkien, *The Return of the King,* p. 382.
19. *Letters,* p. 329.
20. Ibid., p. 237.
21. Tolkien, *The Two Towers,* pp. 219–70.
22. *Letters,* p. 329.
23. Tolkien, *The Two Towers,* p. 312.
24. Ibid., p. 360.
25. Tolkien, *The Return of the King,* p. 216.
26. Tolkien, *The Two Towers,* p. 331.
27. G. K. Chesterton, "The Ballad of the White Horse," in *Collected Poems* (London: Methuen, 1933), p. 261.
28. Auden, *The Dyer's Hand,* pp. 107, 108.
29. Tolkien, *The Return of the King,* p. 273.
30. Ibid., p. 385.

Chapter 6: Elves and Others

1. *Letters,* p. 236.
2. C. S. Lewis, *Perelandra* (New York: Macmillan, 1944).
3. Tolkien, *The Hobbit,* p. 185.
4. Ibid., pp. 189–90.
5. The Harvard Lampoon, *Bored of the Rings* (New York: Bantam Books, 1967).
6. *Letters,* p. 160.

7. Tolkien, *The Fellowship of the Ring,* p. 348.
8. Tolkien, *The Two Towers,* p. 325.
9. Tolkien, *The Return of the King,* p. 299.
10. Tolkien, *The Fellowship of the Ring,* p. 325.
11. Tolkien, *The Return of the King,* p. 382.
12. *Letters,* p. 328.
13. Tolkien, *The Fellowship of the Ring,* p. 462.
14. Ibid., p. 463.
15. Ibid., p. 472.
16. Ibid., p. 473.
17. Ibid., p. 474.
18. *Letters,* p. 407.
19. Tolkien, *The Fellowship of the Ring,* p. 95.
20. *Letters,* pp. 332–33.

Chapter 7: Tolkien's Creation Myth

1. Tolkien, *The Silmarillion,* p. 8; Carpenter, *Tolkien: A Biography,* p. 255.
2. *Letters,* p. 146.
3. Ibid., p. 287.
4. Tolkien, "On Fairy Stories," p. 73.
5. Richard Purtill, *The Golden Gryphon Feather* (New York: DAW Books, 1979); *The Stolen Goddess* (New York: DAW Books, 1980); *The Mirror of Helen* (New York: DAW Books, 1983).
6. *Letters,* p. 206.
7. Ibid., pp. 286–87.
8. F. J. Sheed, *Theology and Sanity*, (New York: Sheed and Ward, 1946) p. 142.
9. C. S. Lewis, *The Problem of Pain* (New York: Macmillan, 1943; paperback edition, 1962), pp. 122–23.
10. Austin Farrar, "The Christian Apologist," in Jocelyn Gibb, ed., *Light on C. S. Lewis* (New York: Harcourt Brace & World, 1965), pp. 41–42.
11. *Letters,* p. 24.
12. Lewis, *An Experiment in Criticism,* p. 44.
13. Clyde Kilby, *Tolkien and the Silmarillion* (Wheaton, Ill.: Harold Shaw Publishers, 1976), p. 59.

Chapter 8: Magic and Miracle in Middle-earth

1. *Letters,* pp. 199–200.
2. Ibid., pp. 87–88.
3. Thornton Wilder, *The Ides of March* (New York: Harper & Row, 1948), pp. 183–84.
4. Algis Budrys, "Books," *The Magazine of Fantasy and Science Fiction,* May 1976, pp. 64–65.
5. *Letters,* p. 146.
6. Ibid., pp. 188–89.
7. Tolkien, *The Return of the King,* p. 372.
8. Tolkien, *The Silmarillion,* p. 278.

Chapter 9: Frodo, Fëanor, and Free Will

1. *Letters,* p. 200.
2. Joanna Russ, "Books," *The Magazine of Fantasy and Science Fiction,* Feb. 1979, pp. 67–69.
3. C. S. Lewis, "On Science Fiction," in *Of Other Worlds* (New York: Harcourt Brace & World, 1966), pp. 64–65.
4. Ursula LeGuin, "Science Fiction and Mrs. Brown," in Susan Wood, ed., *The Languages of the Night* (New York: Berkley Books, 1979), p. 97.
5. Tolkien, *The Silmarillion,* p. 78.
6. Ibid., p. 78.
7. Ibid., p. 79.
8. Ibid., p. 52.
9. *Letters,* pp. 394–95.
10. Ibid., pp. 399–400.
11. Tolkien, "On Fairy Stories," p. 59.

Chapter 10: The Sudden Joyous Turn

1. *Letters,* p. 172.
2. Tolkien, *The Fellowship of the Ring,* p. 71.
3. *Letters,* p. 150.
4. C. S. Lewis, *The Last Battle* (New York: Macmillan, 1956).
5. Tolkien, "On Fairy Stories," p. 49.
6. C. S. Lewis, *A Grief Observed* (London: Faber & Faber, 1961; New York, Bantam Books, 1976), p. 23.
7. Ursula LeGuin, *The Farthest Shore* (New York: Atheneum, 1972; New York: Bantam Books, 1975), p. 122.
8. Ibid., p. 136.
9. Ibid., p. 178.
10. *Letters,* p. 400.
11. Ibid.
12. See, for example, Emile Fackre, "Theology and Ecology," in Ian G. Barbour, ed., *Western Man and Environmental Ethics* (Reading, Mass.: Addison-Wesley, 1973).
13. Tolkien, "On Fairy Stories," p. 69.
14. Ibid., pp. 71–72.
15. *Letters,* p. 413.
16. Ibid.
17. William Shakespeare, *Hamlet,* Act I, Scene II.
18. Tolkien, "Leaf by Niggle," p. 112.
19. Ibid.
20. Tolkien, "On Fairy Stories," p. 73.

Index

Ace Books, 40–43
Aesthetic religion, 11–12
Afterlife. *See* Immortality
A Grief Observed (Lewis), 133
"Ainulindalë," 88, 94
Ainur, 88, 91; miracles of, 114; as
 subcreators, 91
"Akallabêth," 100
Allegory, 16–27
Alternative world story, 109
Aman, Land of, 99
Amazing Stories, 28
An Experiment in Criticism (Lewis), 9–10,
 26
Animistic view, 106–107
Antiheroes, 61
Apollo, 13
Aphrodite, 37
Aragorn, 45, 52; criticism of character,
 120; heroic love of, 77; and Hobbits,
 54; ordinary life of, 79
Archmage Ged, 134–135
Arda, 88
Arwen, 77, 79
Asimov, Isaac, 29; robot stories, 36;
 Tolkien on, 38
Aslan, 132–133
As You Like It (Shakespeare), 22
Atlantis legend, 10–11, 100
Auden, W. H., 24; letter to, 43; on
 servant/master metaphor, 71–72
Aulë, 89, 90
Avari, 99

Baggins, Bilbo. *See* Bilbo Baggins
Baggins, Frodo. *See* Frodo Baggins
The Ballad of the White Horse
 (Chesterton), 71
Ballantine Books, 41, 43
Balrogs, 97; and Gandalf, 114
Barrow-wights, 53

Beauty, 20–21
Belief: and myth, 14. *See also* Primary
 belief; Secondary belief
Bilbo Baggins: beginnings of, 46; courage
 of, 46–51; and Dwarves, 46, 47, 50;
 and fate, 116; and Gandalf, 46, 50; life
 span, 131; and Mirkwood spiders,
 69–70; and Ring of Power, 13, 52
Black Riders, 129
Blessed Land, 73, 122
Blish, James, 34
Bombadil, Tom. *See* Tom Bombadil
Bored of the Rings (Harvard Lampoon), 76
Boromir, 55–56, 61–62, 83
Brackett, Leigh, 33
Bradley, Marion Zimmer, 33
Bratt, Edith, 127
Bree, 52, 54
Budrys, Algis, 105–106

Carpenter, Humphrey, 41, 44, 88
Cave allegory, 3
Cherryh, Carolyn, 33
Chesterton, G. K., 11–12, 14; *The Ballad
 of the White Horse,* 71; *The Everlasting
 Man,* 6–7; on Saint Francis, 66
Christ: Chesterton on, 7; and Frodo, 115;
 and Gandalf, 87; and Mordor journey,
 56; in *Silmarillion,* 101; sorrowful
 mysteries, 57–58; virtues and, 71. *See
 also* Mary, Virgin
Consolation: meaning of, 137–138; of
 religion, 133
Cotten, Rosie. *See* Rosie Cotten
Councillor Tompkins, 19, 20; on beauty,
 21; life after death, 23
Crack of Doom, 57
Creation myth, 88–101

Dark Lord. *See* Sauron
Dead Marshes, 129